Give to Grow

9 Principles
for
Conscious Business,
Social Media
and Life

by

Shelley R. Roth

SPRINGBOARD PUBLISHING

www.springboardworks.com

Jacket design and layout by Shelley R. Roth and Marisol Graham.
Photography by Lea Wie Photography.
Edited by J-Coby Wayne.

LIBRARY OF CONGRESS CATALOGING-IN-PUBLICATION DATA.
Roth, Shelley R.
Give to Grow: 9 Principles for Conscious Business, Social Media and Life© / Shelley R. Roth. - 1st ed.
p. cm.
1. Marketing & Sales 2. Business & Economics 3. Social media

ISBN (paperback): 0-9838704-4-6
ISBN (paperback): 978-0-9838704-4-9
ISBN (electronic book): 0-9838704-5-4
ISBN (electronic book): 978-0-9838704-5-6

PRINTED IN THE UNITED STATES OF AMERICA

First Edition

Sign up for my video tipster newsletter: visit www.shelleyroth.com.

TABLE OF CONTENTS

FOREWORD

Shelley and I first met in Houston during the early 2000s. We were both working on trying to bring more wisdom and conscious business practices to the business world. I had a table set up displaying materials at a meeting of the Houston Chapter of Women in Technology International. Shelley, being her friendly self, was one of the few people who came over and talked to me. We discovered right away that we were working in the same field, coming at it from slightly different angles.

Back in those days, we were both swimming up-current. It was hard and slow going. Over a decade later, here we are, putting out a book about nine conscious business principles with the participation and support of a robust network of panelists and Google Hangout audience members and researchers all pulling together to bring what much of the world is finally starting to realize into an accessible, engaging and practical form. Much of the business world has come to realize that cooperation is the new competition, with everyone from GE's Jack Welch to the *Harvard Business Review* talking about cooperation and collaboration as a "new" business model. Yes, the institution of business is still struggling today with how to "measure" the ROI of cooperation, but in this book, Shelley and the panelists who participated in the Funday School for Business Hangouts that generated the book's material give convincing alternative ideas about what to measure, whether the concept and form of measurement as we have known it is even relevant and a different version of ROI - return on influence.

Many of the corporate "crash and burns" throughout the 2000s that came to a head with the 2008 economic contraction and its aftermath opened the way for business to be ready for this book's more conscious ways of doing and being. With people and with corporations, it often takes a big hammer to create the space and momentum to change course. In conversations with Shelley as her book editor and energy guide, we talked about competition and whether it has any place in this new world since this is a book about giving to grow and being more collaborative.

From an energy perspective, competition is a natural phase and a mode in the shared path of evolution. On the path of evolution, human beings have progressed over aeons of time through stages of individualizing to self-interest to self-awareness to awareness of another to awareness of and identification with family to identification with community and groups (sports teams, one's country, one's company). Many people are now evolving into greater identification with the entire planet as home and humanity as one family.

Just as individual people must go through a phase of self-interest and intense self-awareness to get to know themselves and to hone and develop a powerful and magnetic personality that can later be turned to influential service and doing good, corporations and business are going through the same thing. From an energy perspective, they are laboratories to bring people together and experiment with group dynamics and the processes of turning an idea (energy) into a tangible thing or service (matter).

In this process, competition is a phase. Different people (and businesses) evolve at different rates, and competition is necessary at a certain stage to stimulate excellence. "Healthy" competition is when we see excellence around us and respond to that excellence internally as an inspiration and fuel to better ourselves and raise the bar on our own endeavors and efforts. "Unhealthy" competition is when we see excellence around us and respond to that excellence externally to crush those who are excellent - "the competition" - to better ourselves at the expense of others.

Unhealthy competition has a scarcity mentality, seeing that when one “wins”, everyone else “loses” because “there’s only so much to go around”, thus, when one person or group has experienced excellence, everyone else has failed in not being the one to do it first. Healthy competition is secure, open, respectful and loving of the excellence in others. Unhealthy competition is insecure, secretive and diminishing and destructive of the excellence in others. Healthy competition has an abundance mentality, seeing that when one “wins”, everyone “wins” because a new level of excellence has been brought to the world. In fact, what comes after healthy competition is “grow-grow” collaboration where the concept of “winning” or “win-win” isn’t even part of the vocabulary. This is because in “grow-grow collaboration”, we’ve evolved completely out of systems with their roots in competition into identifying as stewards where the culture and actions center around cooperation and collaboration to bring growth for all at the expense of none.

Much of the unconscious or unethical behavior of business is due to that evolutionary phase of self-interest. Think of a teenager: Often our beautiful, loving, caring, considerate children turn into raging balls of self-centered angst and inconsiderate behavior. They’re not bad children; they are being flooded with the new chemicals and energies and powers of adolescence and sexuality, and it is like trying to hold onto a fire hose pumping thousands of pounds of pressure of water through it. It’s a huge pressure that most people don’t understand in a complete and compassionate context without an understanding of how energy works. Many companies that start out good hit “adolescence” and start behaving like teenagers. They come into contact with the tremendous power and magic of translating an idea into a successful, influential, highly profitable product or service. If they’ve been born with more smarts than heart, the power can do funny things to them and the people who work for them.

Where does competition fit into this? For the businesses and people who are in the self-interested to self-aware phase of life, they need external stimuli to know and activate themselves. Think of many excellent salespeople. They thrive on making targets, hitting the numbers, seeing what the person next to them is doing to motivate them. They love the game, they love the chase. Think of Olympic athletes. They break records because someone has set a record to break. The sales quota, the Olympic record... these are tangible yardsticks for which to aim, and for those whose nature and work are to be very focused on energy in physical form - businesses, athletes, fashion models - tangible yardsticks and points of external comparison are tools for growth.

All people and fields will eventually hit a point in the evolution path where external stimuli are no longer needed to activate the tendency towards excellence. But competition and competitiveness are likely to exist for a while to come - in people, in business - while there is still a need for external prompts towards excellence. And because people and corporations are learning to manage and wield tremendous power and the ability of influence through this process, there will be blips along the way where power distorts. But as Newton said, "For every action, there is an equal and opposite reaction." We might not see the equal and opposite reaction to the distortion created by self-interested, hyper-competitive and sometimes unethical people and businesses in our lifetimes, but we can be as sure that that reaction will come as we can be sure that an apple will fall down to the ground thanks to the Law of Gravity.

The ever-greater trend towards a recognition and valuing of cooperation as an "alternative" model in business is a beautiful thing. It is a sign that humanity and business are evolving past the self-interested phase and are on the way towards crafting beautiful vessels of matter and form to express ideas and energies that are truly useful and good out into the physical world. When business comes to recognize its reality as a wielder of love in the form of money, ideas and influence, it will be an unstoppable force for good. How lucky we are to be alive at the dawning of this reality! The conscious business practices Shelley shares in this book are a powerful and joyful contribution to helping bring this reality to life.

J-Coby Wayne
July 2015

I N T R O D U C T I O N

Give to Grow: 9 Principles for Conscious Business Social Media and Life

"Give to Grow" is the single most important operating principle for both my life and my business. I have been practicing this way of being over the last decade, and without a doubt, it alone has created more abundance and richness of being in my life. What I have found is that this approach has served as a foundation for who I am, what I stand for and what I reflect, both in business and personally. Giving to Grow has enabled me to live better and be happier with less fear and has brought an enormous amount of joy, goodwill and success into my life and business.

This book came about through an idea I had in January 2014, sparked by my experience with Giving to Grow: A monthly online business series using Google+ Hangouts called "Funday School for Business." The series ran for nine months from February through October 2014, and the recordings of those hangouts are still available at www.youtube.com/springboardw. The idea for this series was to gather together businesspeople doing business (and living life) according to what I deemed a principle of "being conscious" in how they were operating their businesses and interactions with others. Each month, we focused on one core "conscious business principle" to help transform the business and personal lives of participants by bringing more fun, collaboration and meaning into how we work and contribute to the world with our talents and interests.

The Funday School for Business format was me facilitating a rotating set of six to eight panelists who would dialogue for an hour about their experience with the principle for that month. Attendees from the public watched the live Google+ Hangout online and were able to interact with the panelists and me through the Hangout's Q&A feature. The panelists changed from month to month, with a core set who participated in all of the Fundays. So much collective wisdom came out of these sessions, I realized it would make a great book, and here it is! What you'll find in this book are my thoughts, the panelists' thoughts and the input of the public attendees through our responses to the questions they asked and experiences they shared. All of the panelist discussion sections in the book are direct transcripts of their own words, with minor editing for flow and grammar.

I want to thank all of the panelists who were a part of Funday School for Business, and I want them and you, the readers, to know it is with their knowledge and contribution that I am able to take this body of work to companies both public and private and bring a fresh perspective to what matters and can be measured as success going forward in business.

Even though the concept for Funday School was born in January 2014, the conscious business practices were something I had been living and thinking about for many, many years as I climbed the ladder in corporate America. All the years spent in corporate America left me feeling empty and void of purpose. Sure, I was making lots of green (money), had great insurance and benefits; however, I knew there had to be a better way... a way that felt right in my heart and didn't leave me with a lump in my throat and a pit in the bottom of my stomach every time I went to work. I knew something was wrong when my manager stated, "We don't pay you to think." Of course, I thought something was wrong with me, but as I got older, I realized there was something inherently wrong with the culture and approach of some businesses in corporate America, and profits were displacing human values.

When I was kicked out of the nest from this version of professional life, I was determined to "bring" spirituality to corporate America. After many starts and stops, I realized I did not have to "bring" anything to anyone. I had to just BE. My spirit would be brought to all I encountered, including businesses of every shape and size, and being human and sharing my spirit would be my opportunity to share my truth.

How lucky I was to have eight years of thriving and providing a very timely business topic - social media - to the masses! It gave me an opportunity to build wonderful relationships and trust with thousands of business owners.

Now, 15 years later, the conscious business practices I have been living and using in my own company were shared through Funday School for Business with other business owners via Google+ Hangouts. It is my intention that by sharing these practical business practices, readers will be inspired to grow and measure success in their businesses in new ways.

Along with my personal experiences of living conscious business principles, many years of training businesses on social media with best practices and navigation of various social platforms helped prompt the creation of the Funday School for Business Hangouts. I have been most excited over the years when I have been teaching and sharing with people the new social media frontier that has really made a difference in my own business, and it certainly has had nothing to do with advertising. It has had to do with building personal relationships, trust and engagement. Engagement has been the new bottom line. If you are "real" and your authentic self online, you have a big advantage with typical corporate players, who at times are hampered by a belief in having to "do" rather than understanding the power of "being."

My goal in creating Funday School and bringing this book into reality is to present, train and speak on the conscious business principles and practices discussed in the book to businesses of all shapes and sizes and to assist them with awakening to the new and improved bottom line for business growth: being conscious, authentic people who operate from the principles and practices of Funday School. I believe this is the future of business, and the true measure of assets and the bottom line. And, of course a by-product is watching your business thrive by being conscious and being yourself!

Many thanks are in order to the village that made this book happen:

- all of the Funday panelists, who are detailed in Appendix II on page 258
- the participants who were live on our Funday school sessions as well as the thousands of people who listened to the recorded sessions
- Heather Swick, who researched, led and managed the interviews of conscious businesses that appear in Chapter 10; suggested several practical exercises; asked good questions and was an early reader
- Kain Sanderson, who gave invaluable insights and suggestions to make this book better
- the editor of this book (and my first two books as well), J-Coby Wayne, who is a force behind the editing and the best energy guide on the planet or in the Milky Way or possibly the cosmos!

- Google+ and YouTube for providing the technology that made the Funday Hangouts possible

I couldn't have done it without everyone's support, energy and contribution.

One of the key ways J-Coby worked with me on this book was to use the amazing tool she and her partner, Kain Sanderson, developed - the "NavMap" - to create the "**Funday School Book NavMap.**" It is the essence of the heart and soul of this book and helped guide how it was created. J-Coby also introduced me to an idea from a teacher, known as "DK" or "The Tibetan," whose wise writings were published between 1922 and 1960 and are still amazingly relevant today. I'd like to leave you with J-Coby's summary version of this idea as you head out on your adventure into conscious business:

> *There is a virtual group of people around the globe who are agents of evolution that act as world servers for the good of all. These are the people who are beginning to form a new global social structure. They consider themselves world citizens. They belong to no party or government. They respect the existence and rights of all parties, all beliefs and all social and economic organizations. They are found in all nations and all religious organizations. They consider that the old methods of fighting, partisanship and attack, and the ancient techniques of party battle, have failed completely. They consider that fighting, violent partisanship of a leader or a cause and attacks on individuals whose ideas or manner of living are different from the masses - and so*

are judged by some to be detrimental to humanity - are out of date and proven to be inadequate to bring peace, economic plenty and understanding to the world. They take their stand upon the essential divinity of humanity and all human beings; their program is founded upon goodwill, because it is a basic human characteristic.

CHAPTER ONE

Principle #1:

From "Win-Lose" to "Win-Win" to "Give to Get" to "Give to Grow"

What started me on the Give to Grow path - and caused me to kick off the inaugural Funday School Hangout with this as our first topic - was how I grew from experiencing the "win-lose" attitude in early business life to more of "win-win" collaboration, then "give to get" and finally, the highest form of the principle, "give to grow", which is where I currently operate.

As early as I can remember, I loved to serve, not sell! I loved business. I remember working with a friend of mine named Nancy when I was 8 or 9. She had an ice ball stand with a block of ice and a hand-held shaver, which she would use to make snow cones that she sold to kids. I was the assistant to Nancy, and I just loved enterprise! This experience is one of the few I remember from my childhood, and it was very gratifying. I always thought this was something I wanted to do - have a snowball truck going around the neighborhood selling snow cones. From these earliest memories of selling/serving, I do not recall being a sales shark nor do I resonate with some of the other terms that circulate in the sometimes brutal world of sales such as "take no prisoners," "eat what you kill," "scorch the earth," "kill or be killed." I just loved connecting people with what made them happy and met their needs.

Unfortunately, my childhood joy met a stark adult reality in my first sales position. After starting my career in education, I shifted into sales, selling frozen food plans. Not only was I selling frozen food plans, I was doing so to people who couldn't really afford them. It was a very rude awakening having to go from being a natural nurturer to having to close deals and having to do a "one call close." Whether selling frozen food plans or direct mail advertising or swimming pools, all were "one call closes" and great training grounds for selling and the "kill or be killed" approach. I happened to be very good at this. But none of it ever really sat right with me. When selling what turned out to be my last swimming pool forevermore, I was discovered by the sales manager of a computer company, and thankfully he saw my raw talent and brought me on to head up a new area of that *Fortune* 500 company.

This company had a heart. It brought me in to "nurture" or farm existing accounts, and this was truly where my comfort was. Now instead of "win-lose" (I, salesperson, win by selling you something as fast and hard as possible; you, purchaser, lose your money and your power in the "one call close"), I could be "win-win" since what I was providing my customers helped them win and me as well.

In previous sales jobs, the customer wasn't seen as losing; they were just seen as part of the competition. It was either I win or the competition (customer) would win, and therefore, "kill or be killed." If I wanted to win, they had to lose. And I wasn't paid to lose; I was paid to win.

In contrast, at the computer hardware company with a heart, working in a channel sales management/nurturer role, I was able to assist my resellers/channel partners with providing the best solution to their customers. It was an indirect sales management role, and I enjoyed helping the partners provide the best solutions to their clients, even though at times the solution I was offering was not the best solution. I knew that I was really good at taking care of relationships, and this was a natural fit. So I became a "farmer" so to speak, and the more I nurtured the land, the more I would be rewarded with a bumper crop. Giving to Grow wasn't in my consciousness yet; however, I was blessed to be at that company that embraced and valued the role of farmer and nurturer, so I could move forward from win-lose relationships to win-win.

The next phase of my corporate life brought me to another *Fortune* 500 company that once again only knew of old models and old ways of selling. It was a pressure cooker, and even though I was once again in a farmer/nurture role with the partners I was chartered to work with, this way of being was NOT embraced by my managers and co-workers. It was back to "scorch the Earth," "take no prisoners" and "what have you closed today?" This behavior was handsomely rewarded with some of the salespeople making millions of dollars on one deal!

I was one of the first people hired that was in the role of building relationships and nurturing the client, but the company didn't really understand this mindset. Even though I was succeeding beyond my wildest dreams financially, the company didn't truly run on this nurturing way of being. They were always a direct sales company with the attitude of kill or be killed. After two-plus years of setting up a brand-new channel of distribution for them, and farming the relationships, they still didn't understand the value of the nurturing/farming. They wanted more sales, more partners, and forget the nurturing! They only cared about closing at all costs.

I was just coming into my own at this time, and I was sharing my intellect and showering management with ideas for growth and building stronger relationships. Ultimately, it got me fired. This was a gift, although at the time, it certainly didn't feel that way! When they came up to me and told me, "We don't pay you to think!," I knew I would have to be gone, and sure enough, they helped me make that decision by firing me! Best thing that ever happened.

From Give to Get to Give to Grow

Our first Funday topic of "Give to Grow" is one near and dear to my heart. Over the years, I had heard of the "give to get" philosophy of living, but it never felt genuine to me. I mean, if I was truly giving in the spirit of giving, why would I expect a "get" in return? That just didn't feel right to me. Being the sales shark that I had learned to be in corporate America (my second book is called *Shedding Your Sales Shark*), I was fearful of giving away anything, even after I moved out of sales and became an entrepreneur. In fact, I spent a pretty penny on lawyers protecting my Intellectual Property in my first entrepreneurial endeavors. Then, boom, social media happened...

About eight years ago when the world of social media was in its infancy, I was lucky enough to jump on the bandwagon and start my own business doing social media training, speaking and consulting.

Like magic, I discovered what I was truly looking for in my progression from "win-lose" to "win-win" to "give to get". Social media is all about "giving to grow" (a term I first heard from my energy guides, J-Coby and Kain). In social media, best practice is not to worry about getting back. In social media, if you come from your heart and give your knowledge, you will attract people to you who want your knowledge.

This was a very hard lesson for me, but it really was social media that helped me open up the "give to grow" floodgates, and "give to grow" became my mantra. Now it brings me such a feeling of accomplishment when I hear others saying "give to grow" rather than "give to get."

Social media is the ideal platform to give without worrying about getting. And so, this is how I ended up with my new way of being, giving and knowing my business will grow... having faith and trusting in the process to just do it!

Another way to think about give to grow is Newton's Third Law of Motion: **"For every action, there is an equal and opposite reaction."** Every action has a consequence. This applies to everything in nature; this has been proven. For every act of giving with no strings attached, giving is extended back to you. Maybe not directly back from the person you gave to and maybe not in the same form in which you gave (for instance, if you give someone money, it may come back to you as health or avoiding an accident), but back from SOMEWHERE and IN SOME FORM in equal proportion to what you gave. This is a law of nature as much as the law of gravity or the law that causes our sun to rise and set each day. So few people actually give with no strings attached that this natural law isn't much in evidence if you look for it. But if you look at the life and experiences of some of the very few people who really, truly, purely "give to grow" in total selfless service with no sense of fear, scarcity or expectation, you see that miraculous things come back to them constantly. Our panelists are some of those people.

In our first Funday School, I challenged our panelists (see Appendix II on page 258 for more information on the panelists and their backgrounds) to share where they had seen "give to grow" and Newton's Third Law of Motion play out in life or business, how they know or believe this is true and how they applied this practice in their lives and business.

I kicked the Funday Hangout off by speaking first and sharing my biggest Give to Grow, which happens to be a weekly social media video tip that I have been doing for almost three years. I love providing this educational tip with no thought of what I will get. Now, some 400 videos and some 200,000 views later, well, my business couldn't be better, and talk about feeling like I am helping others! Feedback on the videos has been phenomenal. When you give up caring about measurement, it all starts to flow because you're just growing.

Here's what the panelists had to say about Give to Grow:

Our Funday Panelists Share on Give to Grow

Our Give to Grow Panelists

Deb Tummins | Executive Coach

"Consistently I have found that everybody wants to feel like they are making a contribution. Whether it's a stay-at-home mom or a corporate executive, everyone wants to know they have contributed. 'The Theory of Reciprocity' is that if you give someone something, they're going to feel like they want to give you something back. For me, personally, it has not been the goal to hope to get something back, but what I have found for myself at this point in my life is that it's really all about giving for me. I feel like if I can wake up any day and know that I can have an impact on one person's success by giving them some ideas that they haven't thought about doing or by helping them identify what they should be doing that they already know, but haven't really thought through, then I've had a great day; I've had a lot of success.

Nothing thrills me more than to give advice for free. When I do that, one of the things that people typically ask is, 'How can I help you?' That's when I say, 'You know what, if some of my advice works for you, and if you've read about my business, if there is someone who comes to mind, I would certainly appreciate an introduction.' And that works tremendously for me. It really makes me feel good because at the end of the day, I think we are all striving ultimately for happiness and connection with other people."

Shelley commented:

As a footnote to Deb's commentary, Deb and I worked at the same company where I had one of my corporate sales jobs. She was a real powerhouse in corporate America and did an amazing job. I wish I had had an opportunity to know her then; however, she was several levels above me, and it wasn't easy to go to the Taj Mahal of those upper levels to see her. The great news is that she's now a client of mine, so I get to mentor her, and she has become my teacher as well. Funny how life happens!

Question from the online audience participants:
"Is there a way to quantify the relationship between giving and earning a living through our business? Can you put a percentage on that relationship?"

Shelley commented:

"I have had success by not worrying about the numbers and going from 'Return on Investment' to 'Return on Influence'. I mean, how do you measure ROI (influence)?"

Deb Tummins commented:
"I also think it's very difficult to assess the percentages. I think influence and giving are more of a philosophy from my perspective. And it's not counting how often we do things for someone in order to get them to buy something from us or something like that. It's more about being authentic about our desire to serve and being authentic about how we want to make a difference. And I think there is a good example of an individual who has had an incredible career from giving. He's successfully monetized it. He's Brendon Burchard, and he's probably one of the best marketers out there right now. You can log onto his website and get into his video program. He shoots out a video every single day on topical information that's very valuable, and it's free. He's ultimately trying to get you to come to one of his seminars or buy his book, which I highly recommend; it's called *The Charge*. But he gives a lot, and he is genuinely authentic about this."

Isabel Acosta commented:
"We all know people are going to buy from people that

they know, like and trust. And that has to come first. As Maya Angelou said, people are not going to remember what you said to them; they're going to remember how you made them feel."

Isabel Acosta | Network Marketing Professional

"As a leader in my network, I have to 'give to grow' continually in order to assist my team in seeing what is possible. It's not about sell, sell, sell. It's about helping people realize their dreams, and as a selfless leader, I am entrusted to guide people in growth. I am a mentor, a coach and a trainer. I give unselfishly, knowing the rest will take care of itself. Word-of-mouth advertising is the best. There is nothing like it... for somebody to say, 'I know someone that can help you' or the other way around. There's just nothing like it. That's the best way to grow our business."

Shari Joyce | Marketing Consultant

"So give to grow is something very close to my heart, and luckily for me, I know people who feel the same way. My life is kind of guided by the Law of Attraction, and another one is definitely the Law of Circulation. It's just as unhealthy to take and take as to give and give. As we circulate money freely, more money flows into our lives. You can only give in proportion with your ability to receive. Always give away whatever it is you want. If you want love, give love; if you want money, give money; if you want knowledge, give knowledge. By giving, you can't help but grow."

Shelley commented:
"What Shari just said brought up for me my thirst for knowledge. I must want lots of knowledge 'cause I truly value knowledge!"

Deb Tummins commented:
"As Isabel said with Maya Angelou's quote, I think giving with authenticity is so important because when you give to people, they feel good."

An online audience participant shared:
"I gave on LinkedIn, and they sent the world to me!"

Question from an online audience participant:
"How do you turn your giving into a business? I give a lot. It comes naturally, and I'm not really comfortable charging for it. My industry is in ministry, so for me there's a fine line just because of what I do."

J-Coby Wayne commented:
"That's a great question, and it's a question that's very typical among people who are working more in the spiritual realm or in the things that are not necessarily so easily quantifiable and are addressed to our inner life. In my experience, especially in cause-based endeavors - which ministry of course is - you have one thing to overcome: that is, a big belief that no one should have to pay for spirituality or 'doing good.' And it's pretty ironic, because how much do we pay doctors and lawyers? And yet we think that because it's 'spiritual' or 'ministry', it should just be free-flowing when in fact the people who are attending to our inner lives and our souls - if we want to put it in that vocabulary - are providing a value that's so far beyond anything that is measured in money. We have to work to get past that belief, and I think that's happening more and more as people are coming to value more of the 'intangibles' as the intangibles become more real.

Secondly, it's always really important in cases like yours, because of dealing with that perception that spirituality should be free, to have people around you who are excited and passionate about the cause you're representing because in ministry, you are a channel of another voice. This is sort of the underlying philosophy and approach and, therefore, that also makes it difficult to ask for money and make it a 'business.' So gather around you and engage champions - people who are good communicators or even who are not necessarily good communicators but who are so real in being able to share the benefits of their experience that you can work with them to become the champions who do feel comfortable asking people to support the good work that you're representing.

A third strategy is to really, really continue to recognize what your project, purpose or cause deserves. To recognize that if your project is bringing good to the world, if you are in the 'business' of helping people and enabling others to grow and your whole approach to life is give to grow (it doesn't even have to be articulated for you because it's who you are and what you're being), then that deserves to be supported. It MUST be supported as a counterbalance to so many of the projects that are still opposite of give to grow whose existence is to be expected; it's just the way much of business is currently run." *(Editor's Note: For the reasons shared in the Foreword of this book.)*

J-Coby Wayne | Agent of Evolution

"My story and experience with the principle of 'give to grow' is very personal. I grew up in a very intellectual family - a very traditional New England-New York-East Coast family - where my grandparents' generation was extremely religious. My parents were not religious and remain unreligious to this day. Growing up in this very achievement-oriented and intellectual household, not surprisingly, I ended up going to very good universities for my Bachelors and my Masters. I accomplished every goal I had ever set for myself by age 28 because that's what I and others expected of me.

But when I got to age 28, I said, 'Now what?' I was at the top of my game professionally as the only expert in the world for a while when the world wide web came around in 1995 on what the impact of the internet was going to be on healthcare. I was being flown all over the place. I was being put up in $800-per-night rooms in West Palm Beach and places like that. I was being paid $45,000 an hour to give presentations on things that I thought were pretty self-evident. I was a dynamic speaker, but it wasn't rocket science.

I was doing really well in the corporate world performance-wise and intellectually, but I didn't play well with others. In my perception, it wasn't really anything that I was doing, it was just that people didn't like me, and I didn't know why. So my mind set itself to asking the question, 'Hey! I think I'm a pretty good person. Why doesn't anybody like me?' The universe responded as it does, and a lot of bad things happened to me and to people that I knew and to my possessions that my traditional intellectual and excellent education couldn't solve. To make a very long story short, someone exposed me to the idea that 'what you give out is what you get back' and that everything is energy. Simple, simple concept!

It turns out that my whole personal and professional journey led me to understand the world of energy with predictable laws... Law of Attraction, Law of Circulation, Law of Repulsion... give to grow... influence... all the points that everyone's hit on during today's panel. Those are actual energy laws. What I've come to realize is that when I understood what I was giving out (criticism, editing, entitlement attitude, superiority complex) and changed what I gave, then everything else completely changed around me in response, and now I'm surrounded by amazing people.

In my work, one of the ways I have helped bring the 'give to grow' reality to life and helped more people and enterprises understand how abundantly energy flows when you are aware of how it works is through our 'abundant exchange model.' When my partner and I co-founded our first collaboration, we had initially been charging traditional consulting type rates for several years - that's the world we had come out of - but we we found that charging a traditional set fee places a cap on the amount of energy that can be exchanged. Because the energy is so priceless, it's so valuable, if you try to assign a number to it - say $250 for an hour's worth of work - you get an hour's worth of exchange, and we didn't want to limit the exchange or the energy that way. Instead, we shifted to using 'open exchange' where people could contribute any amount they were inspired to give to help support our work as an exchange back for their perceived value of what they received from us for their direct needs in the form of online events, online educational materials or personalized energy guidance.

So that's some of my experience with give to grow. I've never been motivated by money, and everything I do is to help other people know their purpose. I've seen that when people are flowing with their purpose and that it's a good purpose that contributes to social good and social progress for all, the money comes naturally."

Shelley: "Thank you, Funday School panelists, for your great contributions to our discussion."

Shelley's Wrap-Up

As with the panelists' experiences, "giving to grow" has just been a great practice for my business. Even in social media, my Facebook page is a support page for other businesses to come and ask questions about social media rather than being designed to sell or promote my own things. This is another example of "give to grow."

I've found that in business and in life, the more you make it about "them," the more it becomes about "you"... In social media, this is through your status updates on your business pages, the email marketing newsletter you send out, the event you host for good, the donations you make in your business and more. For example, my weekly social media video tipster email newsletter is all about helping my contacts in my database do better for their business by using social media. A recent tip I gave was how to reach out to meet someone you want to get to know without having a formal introduction. It was a simple tip on using the "backdoor" on LinkedIn to seamlessly meet who you want to meet, and I reminded video viewers to always remember WIIFT (*what's in it for them?*)!

Another way I give to grow is through working with SCORE (Service Corps of Retired Executives). SCORE is a non-profit organization of retired executives who mentor small businesses and startups. With SCORE, we often offer free workshops that help small businesses learn about marketing and growth. I have also contributed my time to many a company that is in need of guidance but doesn't have the budget to hire me. I am often moved to donate to individuals who are colleagues and in need of either marketing assistance or monetary donations. I am taking this even one step farther with a leap of using the abundant exchange model mentioned earlier by J-Coby for my upcoming workshops on the principles from this book. I will not charge for the talks and the workshops. However, I will give people the opportunity to exchange as they feel inspired to do so. I truly believe that what is given helps you grow and comes back in spades! You give, and you will grow!

Science even bears this out:

Study Finds Giving Makes Us Happy

> People are happier when they give versus receive. That's the conclusion based on a social science experiment that found people who give to charity are happier than those who spend on themselves. *Science*, a peer-reviewed journal, published a study in 2008 that included two surveys and one experi-ment. The first survey of 600 workers showed that those who spent more of their income on gifts and charity reported being happier, while the second survey found that those who gave away more of their profit-sharing bonuses reported higher levels of happiness. The experiment gave money to 46 students with instructions to spend it on themselves or give it away. The students who were told to give the money away said that at the end of the day they were happier.
>
> The conclusion by Elizabeth Dunn and Lara Aknin of the University of British Columbia was "How people choose to spend their money is at least as important as how much money they make."
>
> Chris Tomlinson, *Houston Chronicle* business columnist. December 28, 2014

And, finally, a very wise man once said,

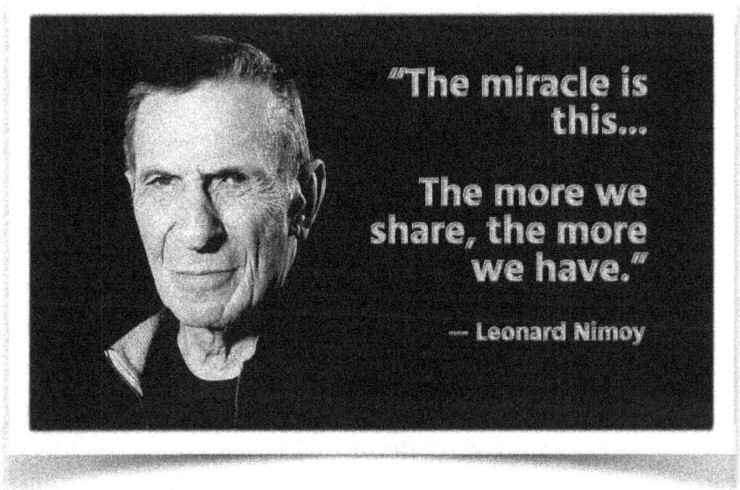

"The miracle is this...
The more we share, the more we have."
— Leonard Nimoy

And that is a wrap on Chapter One, Principle #1: Give to Grow!

C H A P T E R T W O

Principle #2:

From Return on Investment to Return on Influence

Typically we think of ROI as return on investment. However, with the world of social media changing how marketing is done, it has become more about "**Return on Influence.**" Even though this is hard to measure compared to return on investment, it is now a crucial part of business success.

When I say "return on influence," I'm not talking about old-school, sales shark, manipulative influence. I'm talking about how much value and good you bring to the world and to others. So, how do you influence the world and others positively with your presence? What are you doing in the world to bring this influence to life? How can we measure influence?

In more traditional terms, it can be monetary, of course, which is our typical means of measuring the bottom line. It can be measured in how many people see you as an authority in your field. It can be measured in how many contacts you have in your contact base, and it can be measured with how much value you bring by sharing content that makes a difference.

But there are newer ways of measuring influence that are becoming more and more relevant to more and more people and businesses as they seek to make meaningful contributions in the world, largely brought about by the nature of social media. In these more modern terms, influence can be measured by how balanced your life is by happiness, free time, spiritual growth, making a difference, by helping others, participating in local and world issues and solving local and world problems, by making the world a better place and by saving natural habitat in cities (which is what my work is about through offering my donation-based classes, speaking engagements and, of course, this book). There are many different alternative measures of growth or success.

During my 20 years in corporate America, it was my experience that corporations did very much care about return on influence. However, influence for many of them was all about manipulating others by trying to be an expert at control and winning the deal at all costs. This often occurred for me when I would tell non-truths just to assure that I got the order or warded off my competition.

The bottom line was that it was all about getting something back, not about adding value and being influential for the right reasons. Corporate's investment in me dictated that if I was going to invest "their" time, then they expected me to get the next meeting or the order or whatever I had to do to move the deal along. They expected a return on their investment!

At every weekly sales meeting, the pressure was on to discuss what monetary deals were in the pipeline and which we were expecting to close. It was a bloodbath in that "war room" and probably one of the most dreaded weekly activities I had to participate in. The number of salespeople that would basically inflate their projections, or lie, just to "look good" to management always amazed me. And guess what? This is what management wanted, which never made sense to me. I mean, they asked me for a forecast, so I gave a true read on what was in the pipeline. I was never good at telling a lie, so of course I told the truth about my forecasted sales, and often it didn't go well. I just couldn't seem to live the "return on investment" mindset.

In this case, ***I*** was the investment. They were paying me an excellent wage, and they expected a return on that wage. The scarcity mentality, which we will talk about in a future chapter, was alive and well, and nobody cared about anyone else, only about the old bottom line and making money and closing deals. Influence meant wielding power, and it was just an awful environment and not one that was conducive to thriving. Most public companies are pressurized by their shareholders to produce a "return on investment," and the pressure of this flows downhill to all employees. Not a happy place for sure.

When I started my first business, Springboard Ventures Inc., I took my learned behavior and tried to apply it to my new direction. I was advising and coaching start-up companies, all with the goal of raising money from angel investors and venture capitalists. Talk about from the frying pan into the fire! Doing projections and inflating what the start-up company had going on once again went against my nature. Yet I had a successful business doing this for five years. I earned an MBA in real-time learning, and once again, I was a fish out of water, but I was so very good at swimming with the sharks. I even went so far as to start an investment fund with some other partners for early-stage technology companies. Yikes! Thank goodness we never hit our targeted raise of $500,000 for our first round! Otherwise, I may have continued on the path of sharkdom for another few years. Fortunately, social media and my background in education saved the day!

This new marketing medium of social media was just getting underway, and I jumped on board. I was all in. I realized that this was a great platform for living the philosophies and conscious business practices that were at my core. Social media was all about giving to grow, coming from abundance, return on influence, and I embraced all of these principles whole-heartedly.

It wasn't long before I used my education background to create coursework on the top social networks, Facebook and

LinkedIn. My first class almost a decade ago was a sell-out, and I finally had subject matter where I could live my principles and share them with others. The world opened up, and true success was there for me for the first time in my life. I could be myself, my authentic self, without worry of judgement. I could share information and not worry about others "stealing" it. As a matter of fact, I am now flattered when others use my content!

Watching other businesspeople using social media to share content-rich podcasts, humorous videos and other media - both their own and OPC (other people's content) - helped me truly get the concept of Return on Influence. It is all about providing value and doing good in the world. The world is watching, and it is fast to judge, and wow, what a great place to be. Sharing for the good and growth of others.

Businesses that use social media for their own agenda and in the traditional ways of selling are dinosaurs that I forecast will go away. Businesses that don't "listen" to their customers and respond will be judged accordingly, and the days of caring about just the bottom line are going, going, gone! Social media can be very forgiving; however, it can be judgmental as well, so consider this when thinking about return on influence. You are being judged and monitored, so come from your heart, be your authentic self, and you cannot go wrong!

It is refreshing and encouraging to see how we, as consumers, are so much more tuned into companies doing it right these days. Companies that care about the environment, about their communities, about their employees and about more than the bottom line!

There have been many examples out there in the world of social media that have helped me along the path of return on influence, and so far, I have just enjoyed this ride and love helping people and businesses thrive, all while sharing and supporting and not being invested in traditional financial return on investment.

For me, the weekly social media tip videos I send out have a tremendous effect on my ROI (return on influence). When people think of me, they think of an authority in the field of social media. I am an authority, but it is the influence via the "give to grow" principle from our first Funday School that has contributed to this ROI. Being able to not think in traditional ROI terms because I have faith now that the money part will take care of itself, I have been able to focus on giving rather than getting, especially over the last eight years, because the power of social media is not in selling directly, but in inspiring and motivating others. It's about engaging with people, building relationships online and, of course, in person, and naturally, your influence will bring the reward you seek - be it fame, fortune, goodwill, barter or whatever else you use to measure success.

Let's see what our Funday School panelists had to say about Return on Influence:

Our Funday Panelists Share on Return on Influence

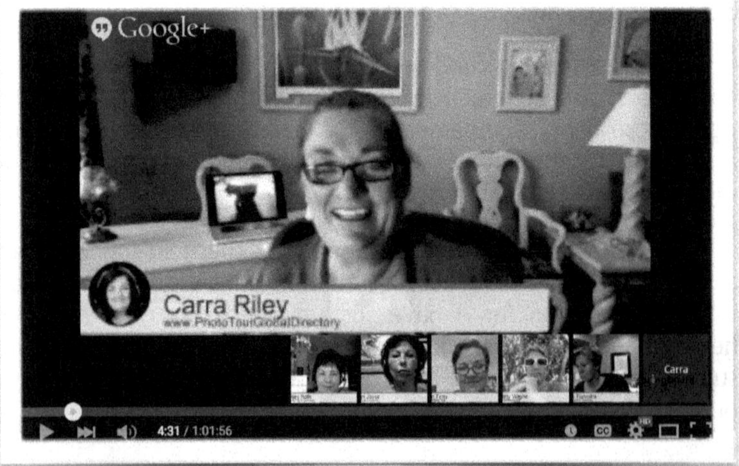

Our From Return on Investment to Return on Influence Panelists

Carra Riley | Realtor

"I really am honored that you asked me to be on this panel with you because we go back a couple of years and this is about influence and I was trying to remember, how did we connect? I think we connected through Mari Smith, who started out on social media. She's a Facebook guru, and she has hundreds of comments on her posts. I went through those posts to see who wrote something intelligent or posted an interesting event in order to discover contacts I might want to friend and learn more about. Shelley, you had written something very intelligent, and I thought you would be a good person to network with and learn from, which I have!

As I got more into social media, I discovered that there are so many beautiful photographs on Google+, so I tried posting some of my own photographs. One person really made me feel like my photographs were okay, and this inspired me to want to learn more about photography. This evolved - like any business product or service in today's market - into needing to have a digital presence. As a result, I have created this new passion that I have for photography into a new website: www.phototourglobaldirectory.com. This is a place where people can connect with photographers to do things like meet up during travels, get help finding local camera and photo shops and create postcards with inspiring messages using your photos while you're on vacation. This is an example of creating positive influence.

I think there isn't a business product or service that can't learn from photography. I think digital images are the currency that opens the door for engagement on social media. As you are posting photos, what a photo says to one person might be different from what it says to another person. But it is that currency of the photos that gets you to start talking. This is just a wonderful feeling. It really is just about investing in kindness and going forward in sharing only the good because you do reap what you sew.

One thing that I would like to say on this topic of return on influence is, when you do connect with someone, go to their 'About' page and their profile on social media, follow them on Twitter, friend them on Facebook, like their page, follow them on Google+ and maybe even Tumblr and Pinterest so that you get a whole feel for them. When you are starting to connect with people for this influence, you want to connect with people who are like you, who see the good and live a philosophy that their glass is always running full and even overflowing! The people that you engage with, the people that you network with, the influencers that you invite into your virtual world, you are in charge of that, so check them out and then support them and share what it is that they do because then you are actually paying it forward."

Pam Terry | Speaker-Coach

"As a speaker coach, I share the idea that it's not about selling anything when you are speaking. It's a time to inspire and motivate others. It's about altering people's lives in some way, to make them better. To influence others is to give to others.

Here's an example: I met this person who is an ex-offender. He was in prison for a couple of years. He was a very shy person who did the Landmark Forum at some point. (Editor's note: Landmark Forum is a three-day personal development seminar program.) Out of the Landmark Forum, he decided to start an organization called 'Becoming One Community' with a mission to reduce the rate of recidivism. (This means reducing the rate of prisoners being released and then ending up back in prison.) Offenders who are released are helped to get a job and acclimate into society again through Becoming One Community. I am going to do a tele-class for him on public speaking, and we are going to charge for it, but all the money is going to go to his organization. This is an example of creating Return on Influence. When I think about Return on Influence, I think I am influencing the world! In doing a telecast for a non-profit - something that you care about - and giving all the money from the telecast fees going back to the non-profit, you are influencing others to give while they are learning something that they want to learn, and they are also helping the organization to grow. You are also helping the other people that are in your tele-class to grow. It is all a state of influence and inspiring and motivation. The return on investment thing, I think, is really so old school. It is sort of like small thinking, and return on influence is big. It is the hottest thing... Look at some fun things like the selfie that Ellen DeGeneres did at the Oscars. The influence that she had! It was the most re-Tweeted picture ever, I think. That's huge influence. And it is causing other people to do it. I think this is such a great topic, and it really makes you think. I am glad to be introduced to it!"

Deb Tummins | Executive Coach

"I coach successful business executives and leaders who really want to be more effective. I choose to work with happy people. At the end of the day, what really keeps me excited about opportunities is really having an impact. My technical expertise is around leadership development and business planning, but what I really get the biggest charge out of is helping people see the impact they can have on others. I think being influential and being powerful in your influence is one of the greatest gifts that anyone could ever have. It is a gift, but it is also something that can be learned and practiced.

Influence can be used positively or abused. I have chosen in my life to use it wisely, and my whole purpose in my work is to really have people pause and realize that every word they say and how they say it will have a huge impact either on a child or a peer or a boss or a board or certainly a lot of people who might read your website or look at your Facebook page or on Google+ or whatever it might be. So I am just passionate about the whole concept of really making a difference and really doing my best to help people understand that it is what they say and how they say it and the presence they have and their awareness of other people and what people need and want."

Shari Joyce | Divine Consultants

"ROI is a common business term for return on investment, usually used for performance measurement and the efficiency of an investment. But I see myself bringing 'spiritual ROI' or return on influence as a citizen of the world of energy and by being aware of how our actions impact lives and relationships.

You can understand a great deal about a person based on the fruit of their life as shown through outcomes and not simply through appearance. Try to think about your life from the perspective of Return on Influence for a day before you post to Facebook or Twitter. Think to yourself, what is the ROI on this? Is it positively impactful? Are they words of power for manifesting good? Possibly your latest rant about the opposite political party is not profitable or directing energy for cooperation. Before you speak around the office, dinner table, on Twitter or at the store, stop and think, what is the return of influence on my words? Are they coming from the thought of world cooperation? Will these words help and build up, or am I just venting instead of seeking under-standing? We have a great calling to be thoughtful about our words and actions, and we have the opportunity to build others up. If we are not mindful of our words and actions, we will have little return on influence and can even distract from our purpose of manifesting good."

Shelley commented:

"I love Shari's input. She reminded me of an app we worked on for my first book, *Get Real, People,* called The 'Real-O-Meter.' It was going to measure how real your posts were on Facebook. It was going to use a scale, kind of like the magic eight ball, to let people who are posting to social media know if their comments were positive or negative influencers. The goal was to make people more aware of how their words were landing on others."

Pam Terry commented:

"When people post negative stuff on social media, we can ignore it by not commenting and not giving it any energy. It's best to post something of value to people. It's about building relationships, and business is built on relationships. This is what social media gives us, an opportunity to be ourselves, that authentic person we hesitate to be sometimes in the business world."

Carra Riley commented:

"I'd like to share a statement from Jack Canfield, author of *Chicken Soup for the Soul*, that he gave at a convention where he was a keynote speaker. He said that he just made this commitment that if someone started talking negatively, he would just walk away. Literally walk away! So if you were dissing someone or you were saying something that wasn't positive, he was just going to leave and not have any part of it. And I think in our consciousness, we actually manifest what we believe. So if we are believing or listening to this negativity, we are taking it in and making it real.

When you think about the big scheme of things, if we are doing what we do in order to make the world a better place, then we have to do good."

J-Coby Wayne | Agent of Evolution

"An example of Return on Influence is that we manifest what we think, what we say, what we do and how we approach life. This has proven to be totally true for me.

I shared a bit of my background in the first Funday School Hangout. In terms of Return on Influence, I was very influential mentally and intellectually, but when I got out in the world and out of the white tower halls of education, I discovered that I didn't really have the scope of influence that I was led to believe I would have based on the Ivy League education that I had. I started to really realize that we do manifest exactly through how we behave, so even if I didn't say a critical word, the energy that I carried into a room was one of appraisal and kind of sizing up. I am an editor in addition to the other things I do - which meant that I used to be in the default mode of interacting with others with an editing eye and editing mind before I was conscious that I did this - and when that is how we are interfacing in the world, I think people feel it, they sense it. They get the sense that they are being sized up, appraised, compared and found lacking more often than not. For me, even if someone was ninety percent good, the editing part would zoom in on the ten percent that needed correcting in my eyes. So I learned about Return on Influence through a lot of hard hammers regarding being understanding and non-critical.

Carra's Jack Canfield story is fabulous because that is essentially how I started on this path of understanding the whole world of energy and the Return on Influence. The first thing I said to my family when I woke up to the reality that energy and form follow thought was that I had come to realize that we had created a very critical environment as a family. I told them that I was not judging them one bit, but I was not going to participate anymore. I told them that if they started to go into a mode of talking negatively about other people behind their backs, I was going to leave the room. I shared that I wasn't doing this to insult them, but that was what I needed to do for myself. So this is an example of Return on Influence - not contributing to toxifying the environment by being strong and refusing to participate in it.

Another important aspect of Return on Influence in my experience is what we define as currencies. Traditional Return on Investment assumes that the only important currency is money. My currency was always making a difference, creating meaning, wanting to solve world issues and problems and helping contribute to making the world a better place, but the currency of influence is different for different people. We can definitely make a sort of universal definition of influence, but I've found in my own work and exploration that there are at least seven different types of currencies of influence and tendencies that people are working with. For instance, a powerful politician is not so concerned with kindness for the most part. That's not their currency. Their currency isn't kindness; it's power. A teacher or a healer's currency is love and their ability to share love and share growth and support growth. For a business-person, their currency is building - whether building an idea, building a solution, building a physical building or building profit - so influence for them is a capacity for and an interest in building. For an artistic person, their currency is experiences. For a technical engineering type of person, their currency is knowledge and understanding how things work. For a spiritual person, their currency is divinity and feeling plugged in to something higher than themselves. And for an organizing and administrative person, their currency is order and structure. I have found that influence and return on influence can be greatly enhanced when we understand the different currencies that different types of people are working with. Of course, we have to start with ourselves. When we know our currency or currencies, we also know where we can have influence and not suffer through trying to have influence where it is not natural for us to do so. We always have the opportunity to become well-rounded but it is actually a Return on Influence to know that there are paths through which we are able to create and exchange more easily than others."

Pam Terry commented:

"Taking a stand for yourself with people who are being negative and taking a stand about not wanting to participate in talking negatively about other people, I think that is great. I've done that myself. On the other hand, when someone is speaking negatively, there may be an opportunity to say something that will transform that conversation. I think there is always an opportunity there because when someone is being negative, that can be a call for help. There is anger there. One way to create Return on Investment in situations like this is to say what is really going on, and see if there is a conversation that can be had to transform the whole thing for that person."

Deb Tummins commented:

"I love what Pam just had to say, and I think that most of us at the end of the day really just want to make a difference in the world and have some impact. We can create greater Return on Influence if we just took a little bit of extra time to think about how we might be better in influencing others, not from an academic perspective, but just by focusing on what we say and how we make people feel. At the end of the day, we may have professions and ways to put a little bit of money in our pockets. But I think most of us wake up every day wanting to know how we can make a difference in the world, and it is very difficult to do that unless you have a way of showing your strength and your warmth at the same time and knowing what really turns people on. We all just have that tremendous power to change the hearts and the minds and the actions of a lot of people just by the way we live and what we say and the examples we've shared. And I've certainly learned this first-hand, thanks to Shelley and the impact of social media. It's just amazing! The different kinds of feedback that one can get just from putting some good stuff out there versus other stuff that others might be putting out there."

Shelley: "Thank you, Funday School panelists!"

Shelley's Wrap-Up

What a great discussion with our panelists in our second Funday School for Business on ROI and Return on Influence!

There even some apps out, such as Klout, that measure how influential you are being in social media land. We have a long way to go for businesses to embrace this new measurement option. However, it is encouraging and refreshing to hear all of the panelists contribute their experiences with this principle. It's truly NOT all about the bottom line, and as we move forward in this book, we interview many companies that are focused on the influence they wield and not only the bottom-line results.

Our next Funday School tackled the topic of coming from a place of abundance rather than scarcity.

CHAPTER THREE

Principle #3:

From Scarcity to Abundance

We had a lot of fun with the third Funday School Hangout in the series on the principle of "From Scarcity to Abundance." We were enjoying the abundance of broadcasting from a very special place - Pointe West on the far western tip of Galveston Island in Texas. J-Coby Wayne was with me live on this broadcast since she had invited me to visit her and share in the abundance of beauty at the beach house she had rented for a week.

An abundance of beauty - view from our Hangout in Galveston

Sharing an abundance of fun with Buddy the Dog in Galveston

The topic for the day was growing your business by moving it from scarcity to abundance. Another way to say this is growing your business by moving from lack to abundance. This is a topic I struggled with all my life, both personally and in business, so this principle is near and dear to my heart.

When I was a sales shark back in the day working at *Fortune* 500 companies, I had a lot of misconceptions about how to do business. This was because the companies I worked for encouraged my behavior to be all about closing the deal, making money and, of course, contributing to the bottom line. At the time, I thought these misconceptions were the right way to do business, and I was very successful at doing business based on their rules and procedures. I traveled the world and went to exotic locations for quota clubs on the company's dime. But, as I've shared, this never felt right in my physical body. I just figured there was something wrong with me; otherwise, why did I struggle so with "their" way of doing business?

When I started my own business in 1999, I still carried these old ways of thinking with me. For example, I would never, ever share a competitor's information with a client or prospective client for fear that I would lose their business. I was coming from scarcity. I also was obsessed with copyrighting and trademarking "my work" for fear of someone "stealing" my ideas. I would never even consider sharing the virtues of a competitor because I wanted all the business. One of my colleagues at a *Fortune* 500 I worked for bought me a button that said, "I want it all!" I was scared that if my clients talked to someone else, I would lose the business. Even if it wasn't the best solution for the client (or a fit for me), I certainly wasn't going to help someone else's business grow.

Now, after so many years of coming from a place of scarcity and not enough, I have experienced that the more I give, the more I grow. As my business and myself continue to grow, and I realize I have it all (abundance) rather than not having enough (scarcity), I have witnessed not only my business exploding, but other businesses with which I have shared the cornucopia of plenty grow as well. Coming from scarcity serves no one and no thing. There is more than enough; there is plenty for everyone. I certainly didn't realize in the early days of my business that there was more than enough business for everyone and that the people that are right for you to work with are the ones that you will attract (Law of Attraction in action!). The big thing for me to learn was, the more I referred people to other businesses, even to my social media colleagues working in my same field, the more my business grew. And it was like - AMAZING! I was like, "Wait... The more I give, the more I grow?!..." Now keep in mind, if you could see my arm, you would see a BIG virtual scar, my "scarcity scar," and maybe it will be with me forevermore because my nature historically has been to come from a place of scarcity and not abundance. What I am sure of is that we truly create our own reality, be it in business or in life, so why not create abundance and give to grow?!

What I have learned in doing social media is that we have so many opportunities to share other people's content via their blogs, podcasts, videos, images, newsletters and even their posts. And it is so easy to share other people's content, whether it is a great blog post or a wonderful video that teaches me something. Even if it is somebody that is in "competition" with my business, if a client doesn't resonate with me from an energy perspective, or I know another company that would better serve the client, then the thing to do is give it away... Come from abundance, there is enough for all. Even when I bring people in to work with me that are colleagues in my same field (what some people would see as "competitors"), two heads are always better than one. So my big lesson is if you really want to grow, you might consider moving from this place of lack and scarcity to this place of "there is enough for everybody." You don't have to worry; you will have enough business if you are doing business the right way. And another by-product is that people will be amazed that you are not threatened by other colleagues in your field. So not threatened, in fact, that you refer them to your "competition!"

When I was in corporate America, there was no community. It was a pretend community of warriors all "fighting the good fight," and yet, the company culture thrived on instilling in us not only external competition, but internal competition as well. That was always the worst part about being in sales, the competing with your own "team!" We were incented to be the top person as the top person always was rewarded financially or materially. I excelled at sales by coming from my heart versus being a great sales shark, and I "won" (earned) lots of stuff. However, I never felt community. I felt competition and that, for me, was not a good feeling to have day in and day out. Being the number one sales rep in my first year in sales at a company with 80 salesMEN and little old me was quite the achievement. But the hate that I felt, the absolute fear that emanated from all those salesmen because I won this fabulous two-week trip to Tahiti, was horrible.

From that point on, I felt like the enemy inside my own company, and everyone sought to beat me. None of this made sense to a person coming from my background in education as a teacher and counselor. As a nurturer and people-lover and giver, this corporate environment was so very challenging. Yet corporate America has thrived on competition, both internally and externally, for as long as big business has been around. But this is so old school. Companies and their leaders that come from abundance like Chieh Huang, the CEO of Boxed and Tony Hsieh of Zappos.com realize that. Chieh Huang has proven it by paying for Boxed employees' kids to go to college. Tony Hsieh has adapted the relatively new management style called "Holocracy" that relies on a lot of self-management and self-organization. This style challenges the traditional top-down approach and leans towards a model in which each employee is his or her own leader.

It is refreshing to read of new directions in business operations. However, much of corporate America is still rooted in the belief that there is not enough, and they must win at all costs. Nature just doesn't work like that. I am not sure why this mentality continues to exist, except to speculate that it is driven by fear and lack. Fear of failure, fear of lack or not enough. And, of course, fear of the investors not getting their money's worth through a return on their stock purchases.

We explore the "new bottom" line in an upcoming chapter where we consider what it would be like if companies had other measurements, in addition to the traditional profits, as part of their balance sheet. I say, why not?! Health, contribution to community, contribution to society, volunteerism, life balance. Why can we not have these as part of our company bottom line and measure them as well? This is where I believe companies are headed, and with great input from leaders like Paul Tudor Jones II of Tudor Investment Corp, the shift will occur, hopefully in my lifetime.

In a recent TEDTalk, Paul shared his concern that our laser focus on profits is "threatening the very underpinnings of society." His talk outlines his counter-offensive, which centers on the concept of "justness." As he states in his talk, "Higher profit margins do NOT increase societal wealth." As a response to this understanding, he founded Just Capital and is creating and implementing the "Just Index" to determine what is important to the public and what is "just" corporate behavior. Beginning in 2015, he will survey 20,000 Americans to determine what they think is "just" in corporate America. Whether it's fair wages or environmentally-conscious products or healthy lifestyles, he will find what America thinks is "just." He will then rank 1000 companies with the Just Index and see how those companies compare with the highest rankers considered the most "just."

Here is a chart from his talk that shows the US off the charts with the ratio of the level of income inequality to social problems. (The US is circled up in the far right corner off the chart and below the chart title.)

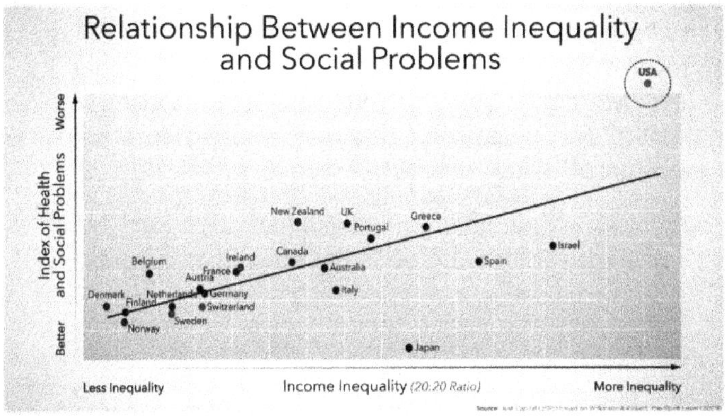

To learn more and see the talk, see:

www.ted.com/talks/
paul_tudor_jones_ii_why_we_need_to_rethink
_capitalism%23t-154657.

When I share the abundance versus scarcity concept in my social media classes, the first thing I ask attendees is, "Do you share blog posts, podcasts, videos, content by other people in your field? Yes or no, and why?" At least 70% of the audience slowly raises their hand and fearfully says, "Well, I am not going to send them to my competitor. Why would I do that?" And this sounds just like my former scarcity and lack mentality self. I can't tell you how many times I hear that when I ask them this question. My response to them is, "Send them there! If they do something better than you, or the customer isn't the right fit for you, then that customer is better served by your colleague. And guess what? If the customer is supposed to do business with you, they will! If they are supposed to come back and do business with you, they will. And if they do business with the other person, that scarcity scar may want to start hurting, but you have to let it go and trust that sharing abundantly will get you much further than coming from scarcity." I have seen this time and again in my business. The most interesting comment I have ever received about this is, "Shelley, we can't believe you put us in touch with your 'competitor' and because of that, we want to do business with you even more!"

Let's see what our panelists had to say about their experience with the theme of "from scarcity to abundance:"

**Our Funday Panelists Share on
From Scarcity to Abundance**

Our From Scarcity to Abundance Panelists

Pam Terry | Speaker-Coach

"What I want to touch on are four things: trust, relaxation, stress and checking your gut. Those are what came to mind to me about this topic of scarcity to abundance. Trust and having faith in things is huge. What I believe in is that giving away as much valuable information as possible to people - that is trusting. I have no problem giving away information because I know that when I work with someone one-on-one, I am going to be able to help them so much more than just giving them the general information. I also believe that you never want to try to sell anything anyway. You want to give so much information that people want to buy from you. I don't like to sell. I don't want to be sold to. So, I am still studying and working on how to present the product where it is not selling.

When you are coming from scarcity, you are stressed out... When you feel stressed out about it, you need to walk away and go do something else. Watch a movie, go play some solitaire, meditate, whatever it is, take your mind off of it and relax. What happens - and this is really cool - is that when you relax, you get ideas, you get inspired, things come to you. Finally, in addition to trusting, relaxing and not being stressed, always check your gut. If it feels good, do it!"

Deb Tummins | Executive Coach

"I am probably an expert on building organizations based on the scarcity mentality because most large corporations are built that way. We also learn about scarcity as children. Many of us are parented that way, and many of us may have grown up with very little resources.

Zappos, the online shoe company, is a great example of a company that isn't coming from scarcity mentality. Usually leaders like Zappos founder, Tony Hsieh, who are focused on core values, happy employees and happy customers, are assuming that there are so many customers out there, they are not leading from a position of worrying about where the next client is going to come from. They have a return policy of a year. Their call service people are discouraged from hanging up quickly. They are actually rewarded if they are on the phone a long time with their clients. Everything they do within their corporate culture is really designed around abundance. They offer every new employee $4,000 after a week of working there, which they can keep or take with them if they decide after a week that Zappos isn't right for them.

If a leader leads from a scarcity mindset, they typically act as if resources are always constrained. They always work from an 'I win, you lose' perspective. They focus on costs and not necessarily benefits. And they focus on 'me', not necessarily 'we.'

In my business today I am constantly sharing information, and I don't choose to charge for it every time. Of course, I'd like to pay my expenses, but I like to share information, and I love to present to people on subjects like influence and leadership effectiveness. I enjoy doing it, and that's a reward to me.

A concrete way that I promote abundance is I would never sign someone up for a yearly training and tell them that they have to pay me no matter what. I am going to assume that I will get plenty of business, and if someone wants nine months of their money back after three months, then I am going to give it back. And I think that is the position that we have to choose to take because people are going to want to work with people who are happy and living from a positive, prosperous perspective versus people who are hoarding or holding back and keeping information. So that's the philosophy that I have, and that's what I encourage other leaders to do."

Carra Riley | Realtor

"What you are all saying is really touching my heart, and I think that is where this principle of abundance comes from - the heart - and if it doesn't come from the heart, it isn't going to work. The principle of abundance flows with the Law of Attraction. The right people will be attracted to you, so there's no need to worry if everyone doesn't like you or your business or your product or your service. As I like to say, 'Some will, some won't, so what, next (SWSWSWN)!'

I think I was introduced to the principle of abundance all the way back in 1980. Larry Kindle was offering a trademark class called Ninja Selling. I was listening to him at that time and applying him to my business career. It was about giving the knowledge and helping the person achieve whatever their goal was. It was all about listening and knowing that the real estate commission, the dollars that come in, whatever it is, is a by-product of your service. That was one of my mission statements back then. It doesn't matter what business or product or service you have to offer; it is all about who you are and knowing who you are and sharing that with abundance. I always ask three questions every day to make sure I am connecting and sharing with abundance: 1) Who was I nice to today? 2) What did I learn today? 3) How am I better today than yesterday?"

Pam Terri commented:

"Carra's comments have reminded me of something I heard recently: Instead of being a 'go getter,' be a 'go giver.' It is not about giving to get something back from that person. It will come from other places. It may not be that person. If you focus on a person you gave a referral to saying that they were going to give you a referral in return, and you haven't gotten it yet, then I think that is coming from scarcity.

Social media and the internet have pretty much connected everyone in the world and have made it easier to come from abundance. They are all about helping each other in any way that we can. And they are also revealing that when you really see something that you want, and you consider it valuable, you will find the money to pay for it.

J-Coby Wayne commented:

"I want to go back to what Carra said about the law of attraction. One thing that people don't talk about a lot in considering the Law of Attraction is that it makes up one half of another law, the Law of Polarity. The other half of the Law of Polarity is the balancing Law of Repulsion. That word, 'repulsion', doesn't always sit very well with people, but it is a beautiful law. The Law of Repulsion basically keeps away anything that keeps you from doing your work and from having a positive influence. It positively repulses or does not attract what you don't need.

Another point is that in order to be in abundance, you have to be good at receiving. For people who are very good givers, like Shelley and everyone on this panel, it is often very difficult to receive. They often feel like the attention is on them, they feel like they are imposing, they feel like they are being selfish when they receive. I had the realization about ten years ago when sitting by the water that the ocean waves come in and they go out, and we inhale and we exhale. Lots of people who are good at giving are always exhaling. They are rarely inhaling, and that's why a lot of people who are really, really good at giving also get sick because they are so busy giving to other people and they feel this guilt to inhale (receive). Receiving comfortably, receiving abundantly; we have nothing to give if we don't receive."

Suzette Cotto | Innovate Social Media

"I took time after a job loss to figure out what it was I wanted to do, so I looked at the question of scarcity versus abundance from a personal level: How was I going to get out of my job loss situation? What was I going to do to make money? I learned over that year of transition that scarcity is a mentality and not a reality. When you think with the 'all or nothing' view of scarcity mentality, it can crush a dream in an instant. When I was looking at starting something from nothing, I had the belief that there really was something to begin with. I also learned to appreciate what I had. I think it is important to say thank you and to give thanks and know that we are not alone in the universe.

It was also important that I took inventory of what my resources were and who my personal resources were and who was on my team to help me through my situation. Another thing that I thought was important was to surround myself with positive energy. If I am going to stay positive and upbeat, I am going to need to stay around people who are not negative and taking me mentally to a place of 'you can't do that' or 'what are you thinking?' You can really bring scarcity mentality to life when you are not surrounding yourself with positive energy.

Another thing that I do is practice daily affirmations. I write them down because there are going to be times when we are having a hard time, and we think that maybe we are going to throw in the towel and say, 'This isn't working.' If you remember your wins and you remember the things that made you take the risk, you are more likely to stay in the game. So I think it is important to say positive things to yourself and to keep your positive energy going. I also believe that your greatest loss can contain your greatest opportunity. There was nothing in my world that told me that I was going to experience a job loss anytime soon. It was a complete shock, and I've never been fired before. Now I am thinking it was a good thing. Getting fired is not the end of the world. Just knowing that where I have come from in the course of a year is amazing to me and is a source of abundance.

The last thing that I think about on the topic of 'from scarcity to abundance' is Shelley's mantra of giving to grow. She absolutely taught me that. I was so amazed that I could go to free classes via Constant Contact and learn about social media. That was the very beginning of me learning how new business operates in the world of social media."

J-Coby Wayne | Agent of Evolution

"I want to go back a little bit to the themes that Deb mentioned with regards to how the corporate world works. I was fascinated to see a couple of weeks ago that one of my friends who is in the space industry posted on Facebook a *Harvard Business Review* blog saying that gratitude is the new will-power. I thought that was amazing. When *Harvard Business Review*, which is about as traditional as you get, starts to recognize gratitude as a form of will-power, then humanity in my view is starting to recognize certain new conscious realities. Will-power is a familiar characteristic of traditional business, but that article is recognizing the will-to-good. And the will-to-good goes back to what Carra mentioned about it being about heart. The will-to-good power of the heart is a fuel of really abundant power. When we come from will-to-good, and we recognize the will-to-good in others even when they aren't always express-ing it or when they are at their worst, that's when the world really starts to change to one of abundance.

A concrete way that I express an abun-dance mentality in my work is the 'abundant exchange model' I shared in one of the previous Funday Hangouts. My partner and I wanted to get off the fee-for-service model, which we perceived capped what was being exchanged. With the abundant exchange model, we don't charge fees for the most part. We ask people to contribute voluntarily to one of our projects that is contributing to the public good. We ask them to contribute what they can and commensurate with what they perceive they receive as value from us. We have more money in the bank than ever not charging fixed fees with a knowing of the truth of abundant exchange."

Shelley: "What an abundant exchange of ideas! Thank you panelists!"

Shelley's Wrap-Up

This Funday School principle was one of my favorites. Such a simple principle, however, sometimes so hard to implement. There is such abundance in nature that is ripe for the absorbing. To know that there is enough for everyone is very freeing and opens a space for energy to flow. Don't get me wrong, I am often challenged by coming from "not enough" mentality. However, I self-correct and realize this serves no one and nothing and is certainly not a positive stance.

So with that thought, we move on to our fourth Funday School session, looking at competition compared to collaboration and what that means to our panelists.

C H A P T E R F O U R

Principle #4:

From Competition to Collaboration

My first profession was in education, and you know, it's funny - I didn't think back on my education life until Funday School. I don't ever remember feeling competitive when I was a teacher, guidance counselor or principal. When I think back to that environment, I remember that there was no real culture among co-workers of competition in the school system. We, as teachers, collaborated and supported each other in many ways. For the students, A's of course were the highest mark they could get, but as an educator, I always found something positive to write on a student's paper even if the "grade" was not perfect. I do think children learn to be competitive in school. Reflecting back, it was a collaborative environment until it was test time or participation time or kick ball time! Even though we didn't have to teach back then to some predetermined testing instrument like the TAKS Test, there still was the competition to get good grades, raise your hand and be called upon and excel at play during recess. As a very shy child myself, I was keenly aware of the "outcasts" and made a special effort to include them in activities. But when I started in corporate America with *Fortune* 500 companies, it was an atmosphere of competition.

If it is competition that you choose to get into like in sports - maybe you are a competitive tennis player - it's okay. In sports, as in much of old-school businesses, there's still a strong culture of crushing the competition. Yet the Kansas City Chiefs football team went from a 2-12 season to an 8-5 season, which they attributed to a conscious shift in their focus to team cooperation - no individuals, no divas.

It's okay to feel competitive if that is what you want and choose and it fuels you without causing you to hurt others. But in the world of business, I personally think it should be all about collaboration. And that's why our topic for our fourth Funday School Hangout was "From Competition to Collaboration." We see collaboration working out there in the business world in real ways, whether it is a company like Dow Chemical Company or Toyota. I learned about how these companies collaborate from a book called *The Culture of Collaboration* by Evan Rosen. He wrote this book to share why cooperating helps your business grow and how getting along is a great culture to have.

Another great example of cooperation is a choir. In a choir, everybody has to sing together, or it is not going to sound good, but you can have a lot of divas in a choir. I've been in a choir and so has my book editor, J-Coby. We've experienced first-hand that there can be a lot of people who always want to be a soloist, but a choir has to be in harmony to really make it work well and sound good. And the choristers who sing out as soloists in a group section that is not written as a soloist part cause disharmony in the sound of the choir. They just don't mesh properly, they stick out like a sore thumb, and they don't produce the sound originally intended by the composer.

Now, in the world of business, operating like a choir might seem kind of hard to do from a traditional standpoint, and I am honestly still struggling with coming from collaborating instead of competing. Even with other local social media businesses, I still sometimes struggle with, "Do I give this to them? Do I bring them into this opportunity?" even though I completely recognize that is the kind of limiting and fear-based scarcity thinking we discussed in the last chapter.

With my old scars from competitive business and sales shark mindsets, rules and procedures, I sometimes find myself slipping and have to go, "Snap out of it!" to remind myself that it is about the customer and not about me. It is about what is best for the client or the customer and NOT me. I have grown three or four social media businesses over the last decade by giving opportunities to companies or referring people to do what I do when the opportunity wasn't a right fit. In addition to that, I try to really remember that two heads are better than one, for sure. I try to work with like-minded colleagues.

I don't resonate with the word "competitor.' It is a negative word to me. Professionals working in my same field and business are not competitors; they are colleagues. And I keep challenging myself to be open and remind myself it is always about the client. Bottom line: I assess how best to serve my customers by asking myself if our energies mesh. And if it's a "no,' then I collaborate with another colleague, or I give it away completely. You can't do everything. You can't be good at everything. And as solo entrepreneurs we sometimes forget that there are always people that we can collaborate with out there. "Collaborate to Innovate" was the theme at a recent conference of event planners where I spoke on social media.

I firmly believe that if we start from a very early age valuing the individual for all aspects of themselves: emotional, intellectual, spiritual, physical, boisterous, quiet, leader, follower, etc., we will instill and grow well-rounded individuals that not only are valued for their "A's," but are also valued for their hearts; not only valued for their outspoken confident contributions, but also for their quiet introspective ways. Having businesses equally value all contributors, including administrators who support the sales roles and everyone in between, will only grow stronger, more collaborative business environments where every employee is valued for their contributions and strengths. Take a lesson from Gravity

Systems, and spread the financial wealth to all, not just to the top dogs and salespeople!

Thinking back on my school days experience, I actually believe a lot of education may not be as overtly competitive as business - although it certainly is in private schools and in the Ivy League - but it still doesn't do a very good job as part of the curriculum to recognize and develop those parts of us and those skills that support collaboration. Schools still mostly teach logic, deduction, facts and "critical thinking." Look at the very nature of those words - "critical thinking!" Those words are competitive and diminishing in and of themselves. Instead of critical thinking, we could say "evaluative thinking" or "evaluative skills" or "observational skills." Those are not-competitive ways of saying the same thing.

And it's emotional intelligence, social intelligence, intuitive intelligence and the intelligence of the heart combined with a refined mind that are needed for collaboration. The mind separates by its nature, so this naturally leads to a competitive, zero-sum approach (in other words, one person has to win, which means everyone else has to lose). The heart joins and unites and seeks common ground and the common good by its nature, so if classrooms aren't teaching or valuing heart intelligence or social intelligence as much as or more than book intelligence, there won't be a culture of collaboration.

Even our early education sets the tone for whether we value cooperation, and since there usually isn't a grade for teamwork, being nice or getting along well with others in public schools, these schools churn out sales sharks, dropouts or sensitive and non-conventional kids who think they are a failure or are less valuable to society. Similarly, in my corporate experience, the high performers always got rewarded. There was one salesperson in particular I remember who crushed his sales number. He was selling ice to Eskimos and whether our solution was needed by the clients he was selling to or not, it didn't matter. He sold anything to anyone without concern for necessity. And this guy was hugely rewarded. He was making hundreds of thousands of dollars on software sales, and management exulted him both with a corner office and eventually a promotion to sales manager. I, at the time, wanted this, but my gut was not in the game. I couldn't believe this guy was being rewarded for scorching the earth and taking no prisoners. He was the example that the higher-ups wanted us to emulate. Folks like me who were great nurturers and relationship builders were not rewarded for that. Management did not care about clients trusting me or respecting me or doing the right thing in selling them products that were the right fit. I did hit my numbers, but I basically got zero respect, and I was a fish out of water.

Not every moment was a shark frenzy of bloodied sales water, though. I had one bright spot of a boss I ended up working with for 15 years. Not surprisingly, he was more collaborative than competitive. He knew how to build a strong sales team with hunters and farmers, and he supported all of us equally in our contributions to company growth. He was a great manager because he came from a place of abundance and never led by intimidation.

On the other hand, I did have one manager who led from pure competition and intimidation. Each person was pitted against each other! Sitting in his gut-churning meetings was grueling for this heart-based salesperson. He had a great talent for belittling and making each of us squirm. He didn't care about collaborating and helping us succeed. Certainly, this was not a place to grow people!

You can always tell the culture of a company by who is rewarded: the high performers who hit or exceed their targets, close the deals, go to the strip clubs and play the game? Or the kind relationship builders with good hearts who are able to close deals, but don't think of it as closing deals? Or the secretaries who always remember everyone's birthdays and kids' names? The question becomes, how do we help business start to value high performance guided by a strong heart?

I think it starts with a business culture of doing the right thing for the customer and the community. Companies that are driven by customer service, such as Zappos, where you can return a pair of shoes for up to a year without question, or REI, where you can return anything forever with no questions asked, set an example of company values on a very basic level. Companies that contribute to non-profits both financially and with time by encouraging employees to use company time to give back are setting the tone and direction for conscious-mindedness.

Having my own business has allowed me the opportunity to get back to my true nature, which is collaborative, and to come from my heart in all my decision-making. This is who I am and who I want to be. It isn't easy sometimes, as I have to walk away from business that doesn't feel right to my heart. However, I would not trade who I am and who I have become for all the financial reward I so sought in my earlier sales shark days!

Let's see what our panelists had to say about our theme of "from competition to collaboration:"

Our Funday Panelists Share on
From Competition to Collaboration

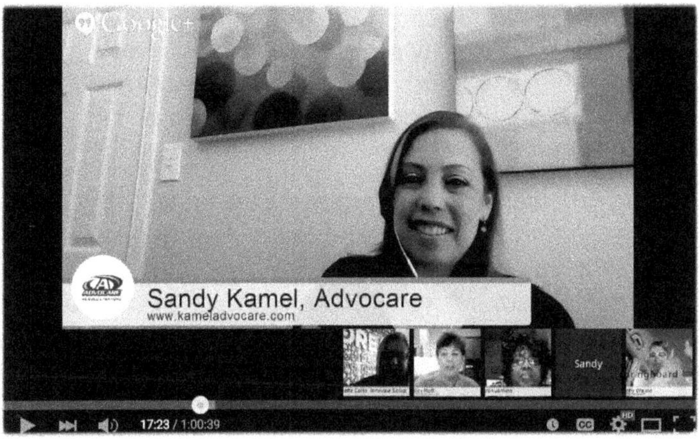

Our From Competition to Collaboration Panelists

Sandy Kamel | Advocare Independent Distributor

"I want to share an experience I've had with networking groups as it relates to competition compared to collaboration. I've gone to a couple of networking group meetings, and what's funny is that I had to reach out to a bunch of groups to see if I could join because most of them are exclusive. They only want one health and wellness person, one realtor, one personal coach. The one that I ended up with is not exclusive. They go with the belief that they are here to help everybody.

I am working on making Advocare my full-time job, but for now, my day job is with Dell Computers. I do reporting. The difference between corporate America and something like Advocare in terms of competition is just huge. When I started with Dell, the performance review process was set up so there were excellent, good and fair ratings, but Dell managers could only give an equal amount of each rating. So suppose you had an awesome manager, which I did, and he hires great people who consistently perform at an excellent level. He still has to give people lower ratings to even it out. This obviously doesn't motivate you very much!

In my opinion and experience, competition can toxify the environment and play with relationships when the focus is just on winning. Then you start to see the people around you as obstacles to your success rather than as colleagues. This really takes away from the common good and the progress of the team.

In contrast, with Advocare, you often hear people say that 'teamwork makes the dream work' and when I win, and my leaders win, and my team wins, and everyone wins, there is a common goal and we all strive to support each other and improve ourselves and our businesses. We take our ideas from each other, and we adapt them to fit our style and personality. This opens up all different ways of doing things. When I don't know the best ways to do things, I can call my team to see if something is a good idea. One thing that I heard from my team leader at Advocare that I really love is that if you are the smartest person in the room, you need to find another room."

Suzette Cotto | Innovate Social Media

"I started my career in technology. I was in management for a wireless technology company, and we built the Internet backbone. So I got to feel what it was like to be a part of a start-up, actually several start-ups. And I think the thing that impressed me the most about the company was that they had a room, and it was called the war room. It had "WAR ROOM" written in black and white letters on the door. All the managers would file into the war room, and there would be this giant white board, and we had to create the internet on this giant white board.

We were people from every walk of life, especially technology people, with very different communication styles. We had to come together to map out a strategy for how to make our services work so that we could work with other companies. The war room was a place where the company provided us with lunch, dinner, chair massages, dry cleaning services, different perks at work so that we would never leave!

Part of that was a feeling of being part of a family of people who stuck together, who were working hard together, who were making personal sacrifices to get something done. At that point in time, we saw the importance of collaboration. Fast forward to now and we have people who don't even pick up the phone because they don't know how. Everybody is busy texting on their phones or talking in an email, and we do very little face-to-face communication anymore. I think we have lost something in that translation. Yes, it is convenient. Yes, we can filter the information that we want to. But unfortunately when we do that, we miss out on things that might be really useful to a team. So I think it is important that today's teams are 'inside teams' that do not think of their teammates as competition and that work together to find a solution to whatever it is they are trying to resolve.

I think that is why I love social media so much because I can talk to anybody I want. I can post any questions, any problems, by throwing them out there on Facebook. If I have a business question, I'll go on LinkedIn and say, 'You know, I heard about this new servant leadership technique - has anybody used it, do we know what it is about?' So that is what I see about collaboration compared to competition. I've never been a competitive person. I'm self-competitive, but as far as being collaborative with other people, I feel like one of those rare people who feels like they want to collaborate with everybody."

Shelley Roth commented:

"I, too, love social media so much because it is a cup of collaboration and cooperation. Thanks for reminding me!

Sharon Jenkins | Author, Editor, Ghostwriter

"I want to focus on sharing my experience in the military for this topic. In the military, we had a different mission and a different purpose from what our public school systems and our colleges prepare us for. We were very mission-focused in the military, and we were very collaborative. If you didn't work as a team when you were in a battle situation, you knew that somebody wouldn't go home because you put yourself before your brother or your sister. I learned how to be a better collaborator, believe it or not, in that military environment. I learned that my strengths are not my limits and that my weaknesses are not my limits. My limits are what I think in my mind. I learned that from fueling other people and seeing them achieve things that I didn't even think were possible for them.

In the military, if you get a command, you have to do whatever the commander is telling you to do, whether you feel you are equipped or not. You don't have a choice in the matter. So it causes you to stretch to get along with the people that are in your immediate circle who help you to bring about that vision or that plan to successfully complete the mission. And you have to have some kind of empathy or sympathy in that mode because if you don't, that competitive nature will come in and devour you. And that is not a good thing. I wouldn't want my life to be on the line and not be able to trust the person beside me.

I believe that collaboration is critical in the business world as it is in the military. When I am in a competitive environment, I don't like me. I do not like what it makes me think, I don't like what it makes me do. There is a place where competition is healthy, but I don't think that we know where that is anymore. So I'm one of those girls who is like, 'Let's get together and let the team do it, and let's make it happen.'"

Shelley Roth commented:

"Isn't it interesting that corporate America models itself after the military, and many of us in corporate work environments feel like we're at war internally? When I feel fearful of collaborating versus competing, I remind myself that Houston is a huge city, and there is enough for everybody!

J-Coby Wayne | Agent of Evolution

"I discovered through a long and difficult path that I am a very collaborative and support-oriented person by nature, but I came up in a hyper-competitive environment. The thing is, I am a very, very good competitor as well. I did very well in the competitive world. I rode horses competitively at a very high level from a very early age. I grew up in a very intelligent family where we were really encouraged to be smart. I came up through Ivy League schools and private schools and excellent public schools where the culture was totally contrary to Sandy's comment of 'if you think you are the smartest person in the room, you better leave and find yourself a different room.'

That wise comment from Sandy is the exact opposite of the culture that a lot of highly intelligent people grew up in. I grew up in an environment where you strive to be the smartest person in the room. If you are not the smartest person in the room, there is something wrong with you. You are not working smart enough, you are not working hard enough. And failure was totally not an option.

Continuing on this theme, I was in Ojai, California a couple of weeks ago hiking. We passed a bunch of college-aged kids walking in the other direction, and I think they were educators. They were talking with each other about what happens when kids are complimented for being smart as compared to what happens when kids are acknowledged or complimented for making a great effort. They were talking about the contribution that is made to others when you make a great effort.

There is such a subtle culture and reorientation towards true collaboration in acknowledging effort and then acknowledging what that effort brings to everyone who is touched by it. It is so different than complimenting someone for being smart. Basically someone is born intellectually smart. You can make yourself smarter in other ways like social intelligence or street smarts, but there are certain genetics that we are born with, so complimenting someone for being smart is like complimenting someone for having green eyes or nice hair. So what, you're smart. The important question is: What are you going to do with it?

Another way we can move more from competition to collaboration is to change our thinking about 'win-win.' What is beyond 'win-win' is 'grow-grow.' When you are talking about 'grow-grow,' there is no competition, no winning or losing. Everybody is growing. If you are faced with a series of scenarios, choices or even a sales situation, what is the sales outcome that creates growth for all involved and for all impacted? This is subtle, but it is huge. It is a complete shift in psychology.

Having a basecamp in Lake Placid, New York when we aren't traveling, I think about competition pretty frequently. I wanted to go back to Sharon's point that she thinks we don't know where the healthy line in competition is anymore. Lake Placid is an Olympic town. In sports, everything is thought of in terms of winning or losing. But the reality is that what another person does for us when they are running or skating or riding or swimming alongside us is basically giving us that extra push and that extra fuel to help us tap into more potential and more energy than we have on our own. There is a greater energy that comes from a group. When you have six people running, that is six people's energy pushing the whole field ahead.

I think the 'line' with healthy competition is where it provides an environment for people to be like sounding boards and mile markers that help us go further than we think we can go ourselves. True sportspeople recognize that everybody wins when someone breaks a record because that provides a new goal post for everyone to aim for. This is the type of healthy competition that helps raise the excellence in all involved.

In contrast, excessive competition almost always comes from some sort of insecurity. When people feel secure, when people feel that what they are bringing to the table is of value or is contributing something, competition naturally goes away. Excessive competition in the corporate environment comes from that sense of, 'I have to win because if I don't win, I am going to lose.' It's Sandy's Dell example. Nothing against Dell - I've had Dell Computers - but, how can you have incredibly smart people come together in a corporation and create a situation where a manager has to divvy out excellent, good, and fair in equal distributions, even if everyone on the team is excellent? It's totally opposite logic.

The corporate world uses and focuses on mental power a lot, but the nature of the mind is to separate, that's how it works, physiologically. When you over-use the mind, it creates division and separation, which naturally leads to competition among smart and clever people who start hoarding information as their key to being one up over the next person. The nature of the heart and the intuition of the soul, if you want to put it that way, is to unify so they are part of the solutions to overcome destructive hyper-competition."

Sandy Kamel commented:

"I really appreciate what J-Coby said. Many of us are brought up that you need to be the smartest one in the room. I think it can affect your self-esteem and create problems when you are not the smartest person in the room. When you don't get that excellent rating at Dell, it does affect your self-esteem, it does affect your security, your feelings of insecurity. If the goal is to grow, not to be the smartest person in the room, then all the emphasis on being smartest is counter-productive in my opinion."

Shelley: "Loving all the collaboration here! Thank you, panelists."

Shelley's Wrap-Up

So, this panel discussion opened up a lot of sharing and collaboration with the panelists. It is an interesting discussion on when competition is good and when is it not. And, for me, I have often wondered why we have never measured common sense! I was always blessed with a lot of common sense, and this is something often overlooked in our school systems and business world. We have measurements for IQ (intelligence quotient), EQ (emotional quotient or intelligence), even SQ (spiritual quotient or intelligence). How about some way to acknowledge the value that common sense brings to the world of collaboration compared to competition?

With that thought, let's look at our next Funday School session, which explores the differences between "business as usual" and "business as purpose."

C H A P T E R F I V E

Principle #5:

From
Business as Usual
to
Business as Purpose

"From Business as Usual to Business as Purpose" was the tagline for the all online Funday School for Business Google Hangouts. It certainly is a mouthful! However, I can net it down to the meaning it has for me. I realized when I was teaching social media classes that what got me most excited and had me feeling most useful and like a "change agent" (that's an oldie but a goodie!) was when I was sharing principles that I was using in my own business.

When I was explaining how these principles were applied with Facebook or LinkedIn, the light bulb would either go off or the popcorn kernel would pop, and some business folks would get it. It always made me feel like I was making a difference when I would hear them use some of these principles in their own businesses and then use social media to share them with other businesspeople. This still excites me almost a decade after sharing them!

Now to set the record straight, I was one of the last kernels in the bag to pop, and in the early days of my career, I really didn't even consciously consider these principles or practices. For me, I was thinking it was all about power and money. Those were the examples I had with a salesperson father and working in corporate America. The minute I finally "popped," I realized that when I gave up worrying about making money for money's sake or gaining power by being promoted to management, and all the other baggage that comes with corporate trappings, I started attracting what I wanted, valued and needed.

What did I want? Love, acceptance, respect, growth, making a difference, which I think is basically what we as humans want at our core level. When I started reflecting that and being that, I attracted that to me. With that came "abundant exchange" - be it in the form of money, barter, volunteering, etc. It comes back to Newton's basic law of "for every action, there is an equal and opposite reaction." It is a basic universal truth.

As I was preparing for the "From Business as Usual to Business as Purpose" Funday School Google Hangout, I received a new book in the mail written by one of my clients, Tom Ferguson. In this book, *Peerless: Defy Convention, Lead From the Heart, Watch What Happens*, I realized that is it in a nutshell. Business is not about what you sell or do, but what you stand for. Putting the heart in sales, so to speak. I might not be the best social media trainer and speaker in the world (although I have been told I'm pretty darned good ☺), but I know what makes ***me*** the best version I can be as a social media trainer and speaker:

- being my sincere self
- coming from my heart
- caring about others
- taking time to listen
- honoring other human beings (and nature)
- giving back through abundant exchange

This is what makes me unique in the field; that's what makes me a success. I can have all the social media knowledge in the world, but what makes me Shelley is being who I am without thought to gaining power or money or coming from scarcity and competition. So those of us who set out to make meaning are much more likely to succeed than when we set out to make money or seek power.

I watched Arianna Huffington on Oprah's Super Soul Sunday, and she talked about her book, *Thrive*. In it, she describes how she was so all about making money and wielding power and that was what motivated her to get up in the morning. It took her passing out at her desk at work and waking up in a pool of blood for the kernel to pop and for her to start questioning, "Wait a minute. Power, money...What is success all about?" So she came up with what she calls "the third metric." Here's some of what she said during the Super Soul Sunday show:

> "
>
> *Our relentless pursuit of the two traditional metrics of success are money and power and it's led us to an epidemic of burnout and stress-related illnesses, and an erosion in the quality of our relationships, family life, and ironically our careers. And being connected to the world 24/7, we are losing our connection to what really matters. Our current definition of success is literally killing us. We need a new way forward.*
>
> "

So this new way forward is the third metric she refers to in her book, *Thrive*. It includes our well-being, our ability to draw on our own intuition, our inner wisdom, our purpose, living our purpose and honoring our sense of wonder and our capacity for compassion and giving. She goes further to talk about commemorating somebody after they pass. Have you heard people memorialize the quantity of likes on their Facebook page or how great their marketing newsletter was or their monetary success or the big house they lived in? Our eulogies are not about hitting those marks; they are about what matters most. As Isabel Acosta and Deb Tummins shared in our first Funday School on "Give to Grow," Maya Angelou said, "People won't remember you by what you say or do, but by how you made them feel."

Now let me define what I mean by "business as usual." In the traditional sense, companies can be driven by the almighty dollar where employees come second to profits. This mentality leads to the "business as usual" model of competition and sell, sell, sell. Coming to work, I would always be afraid. My physical body, if I had listened to it, told me to walk in the other direction. I believe the majority of others felt that way. Even though the company offered coursework as a perk, gym facilities to use, restaurants on site, a bank, a dry cleaner and more, it never felt right to do anything but sell or work. We always felt "guilty" taking advantage of any of those perks. Yes, the company gave us training and invested in our sales skills; however, I never felt cared about or honored for my innovation or thoughts or common sense.

Even when I was making my sales numbers and hitting my quota, it was never enough. You could never relax. It was almost like having to punch a clock. They owned every minute of your life and then some. And they really communicated the true culture and expectations when they fired me - even though I was in the top 5% of quota - because I was questioning, and the questioning was unacceptable. You played a role, and they didn't expect you to stray from that role you were assigned or to be creative in any sense.

This is a typical traditional company. Do the exact job, get your paycheck and get your growth elsewhere. We were not rewarded for volunteering outside the company or mentoring our fellow sales colleagues. We were in competition with them. During my 20-plus years in the business-as-usual arena, I never felt like I was fulfilling a purpose. Sure, when I used my innate nurturing skills to listen to clients, prospects, colleagues and co-workers, I was purposeful. However, this behavior was certainly not encouraged or rewarded. I often questioned, what is my purpose? Certainly it wasn't to make lots of money and climb the career ladder. Both of those left me feeling unfulfilled.

Business as usual doesn't just happen in business; it happens in schools as well. When I was working in schools, it was coming to work at the same time every day, definitely punching a clock, delivering the same coursework from the same textbooks and making every individual fit the same mold. Business as usual was having to pay attention to the edges instead of the middle. It was always the very intelligent kids or the rebellious kids that got the attention. It was never the kids like me - the quiet, unassuming, non-verbal. These kids got ignored. It was the disruptive kids who got the most attention. It was the most challenged kids. It was also the very participatory kids who raised their hands a lot and always spoke up. The average kids flew under the radar. I had 35 students; how could I possibly address the individual? In this type of school setting, the culture and the classroom setting have to be generic.

This isn't an environment of thriving. To me, it's just a sallow field. There's no enrichment. You never have an opportunity to discover because nothing really feeds you. When I was teaching, there was no opportunity for growth. If you couldn't get attention through being smart or loud and disruptive, you just sort of floated along with little direction or inspiration. In my opinion and experience, most education doesn't create individuals. You can't really discover your purpose if you can't discover and express yourself as an individual.

In corporate, business as usual perpetuates this giving the attention to the people who are the loudest and sell the most. Those super salespeople are probably often the kids who were disruptive in the classroom. I remember one guy I worked with. He got promoted to CEO of a huge company. This guy was the kid in the classroom who was just obnoxious. He was loud. He was "take-no-prisoners" in the corporate world. He would sell to anybody. There was no heart in the matter. He would sell even if you didn't need it. He got the corner office. He was promoted, and I just didn't get it. My heart was screaming, "Wrong, wrong, wrong!" It made me insane to sell just to sell, even if it wasn't the right solution. But here was the disruptive kid getting the attention for that bad behavior that made me feel so bad. In school, the reward was getting the teacher's attention. In corporate, the reward was the financial bonuses, trips around the world, the corner offices, the promotions.

Over time, this has a really negative effect. I observed in my corporate days that men, in particular, would deteriorate and decline physically - balding, health issues, drinking way too much, no room for creativity, no fun. For me, it was really horrible. I never fit a traditional corporate or lifestyle mode, and not only did I not want to do all the drinking and competing and having no fun or balance, I never felt like I could talk about personal life and bring my real self to the table. For me (and others I worked with), it was "put on your game face." Time to take the mask out. Time to go into battle. You had to act the part unless you could thrive naturally in that environment. Maybe for the people who do thrive in that environment, they are naturally competitive, and maybe the corporate environment is familiar and no big deal. I know someone who played competitive tennis, and she was happy and always smiling in her corporate work. I knew a few people who were in their right element in the traditional corporate environment, but they were the exception. They were ethical and principled. They were allowed to think. Some were in senior positions. Some were on the same level I was on. They never seemed affected by the pressure. Maybe they already came from a place of abundance or had money or had power or were on purpose.

But to me, it always felt like you had to check your real self at the door. This is generally a good indicator that you're not on your purpose! For those who love and thrive in the traditional corporate environment, that's great. However, I do believe this book is pointing to a better way that can accommodate typical "alpha" achievers who are fueled by healthy competition, targets and financial or status rewards AND nurturers who are fueled by cooperation, relationships and the greater good.

Business as purpose is something completely different from business as usual. Business as purpose is when a company goes beyond a myopic view of what success is. These companies care more about a global view - not just inside the company, but outside the company as well. The outdoor clothing company, Patagonia, has what it calls "planetary goals" out to 2050. Other examples of business as purpose include creating productive teams inside the company for the betterment of the company by bettering the community, local or worldwide. These teams do things like brainstorm where the company can volunteer or donate at the holidays and how teams can be structured to be more collaborative.

A company that's purposeful doesn't focus only on the bottom line, but they do view generating profit as one of the important and powerful ways they contribute to the community and society. They recognize that profit is often supported or enhanced by other assets and some of the types of non-monetary currencies our panelists shared in early Funday

Hangouts. Some of the other assets valued by business-as-purpose companies in addition to profit include:

- time invested in doing good in the world or community;
- the health of the employees being encouraged by working out and being proactive in their healthcare needs at work instead of being worried about wasting time;
- how much of the profits are being contributed to non-profits.

Now let me define what I mean by "purpose." When I think of purpose, when I am on purpose, it feels good. It usually has to do with me getting out of the way and just being and doing and knowing that when you are on purpose, your ego is not involved.

Discovering your purpose isn't always easy. I don't think you can find it like a lost watch. People who are fortunate discover their purpose early on. I didn't know what my purpose was until I got back to my roots and started teaching/training again. It came so naturally. It was so gratifying. It filled my soul and my spirit. It's almost like an instinctive thing. I thought my purpose was making money, was saving money, was climbing a ladder, but none of those ever felt good. They never fed my soul. How I discovered that was through some coursework that helped me remember that I am a pied piper who naturally leads people through my "pied piper" song (my joy in teaching and sharing information) even though I don't set out to lead when I teach or share.

I remember when I was young, they said I was a pied piper with children. I never understood this. I never really considered myself a leader, but I opened my nurturer's heart, and now I understand my purpose in this world. When I am teaching social media classes (and soon to be the principles from this book), I am helping others and giving them permission to be their true selves by being my authentic self. This is my purpose.

To get at your purpose, keep asking yourself and exploring what it might be. Dedicate and schedule some time each week to being quiet and letting it come to you where you are most comfortable, where you don't have to think. Where's your muse? Where or what do you get inspiration from? Sometimes we have to still our minds enough to be open to hear it. Keep listening to your body; if it doesn't feel good, it's not your purpose.

Another way to get at your purpose is to take courses or work with coaches or advisors that focus on ways to get closer to your purpose. There are so many out there these days! Just search online and in social media, and see what speaks to you. There are different types of language that point to different kinds of approaches, and you'll resonate more with the language that's right for you. Some approaches are centered on personal or professional development; some approaches are mystical/spiritual or based in religion; some draw on principles of psychology, interpersonal relations and communications; some are based on the view that everything is energy, and just as physics creates predictable happenings and outcomes (as we shared early on in the book with Newton's Third Principle of Motion - "for every action, there is an opposite and equal reaction"), if we know how energy works in business and in life, we can easily access the blueprint of our purpose that already exists within us. I've written three books with a lot of catalyzing inspiration from my energy guides, J-Coby and Kain, who often reveal to me deeper aspects of things I know, but don't know I know.

When you meet someone who is on purpose or deal with a business as purpose, you know it. They make eye contact more frequently. They listen intently. They truly care about others. They're very much in tune with call it "spirit," faith, God. They are very much in tune with a higher power or being part of something bigger than themselves. They have wonder. They're the ones that get and live the 9 principles in this book. They have often learned some version of the 9 principles at an early age, sometimes through church. They're selfless in a sense, always thinking about the greater good and serving others, being in learning mode, seeking noble role models and aspiring to be role models, being aware of how their words and actions affect others and the community and society at large.

But they also take care of themselves and know that it is not selfish to attend to their well-being and do things outside of work that fuel their purpose, good health and happiness. They are committed to the recognition and reality that if they are not healthy and happy and on purpose, they are not ultimately useful to anyone else in the long run. They understand that when they are healthy and happy and on purpose, they stimulate others around them to be healthy and happy and on purpose, simply through their presence.

When a company comes from customer service first, that's an indicator that they're a business as purpose. We've already shared the great examples of Zappos.com and REI. When a company supports good causes and gives back through their whole way of doing business, that's an indicator of business as purpose. At TOMS shoes, they started the whole cause-based "buy one and we'll give one away" movement that's becoming more common among conscious businesses. Another indicator of a business as purpose is companies that reward employees for contributing their time to the community, whether all through the year or at special times like holidays.

How Social Media Supports Business as Purpose

Social media has opened up more opportunities than ever to be more than just your business and to share your purpose and your passions, build value and create meaningful communities that enable lasting relationships. The indie singer and author of the book, *The Art of Asking*, Amanda Palmer, got a lot of flak for using Kickstarter to be the first musician to raise $1 million to finance her album and her tour while still asking musicians to volunteer to play with her on that tour after raising that money. What the mainstream media didn't understand at all was that Amanda Palmer is a relationship and community builder even more than a musician, and she has a fan base and musician-collaborator community around the world who considered themselves her family long before the Kickstarter campaign. Her global family is a dedicated family because her music is often about being lost, being a misfit, not fitting in, not being understood, and from day one, she realized she could use her blog and Twitter to respond to every single person who reached out to her online and in person at concerts to share their stories of abuse, addiction, mental or physical illness, being bullied, death, suicidal thoughts, being dumped, being kicked out of the house for being gay or transgender.

Not only has she always responded to all this pain and loss in a very personal way, she's also been totally transparent in sharing her foibles and challenges all along the way. In doing this in a completely genuine way, she has made her fans and community of collaborators feel like she is their great sister and best friend because she feels like everyone in the world is her sibling and friend.

In her relationship with musicians, it has always been about providing mutual opportunities to jam. It's always been about making the music, not about inserting money into the exchange, and that's gone both ways. But she's also always been clear-eyed about what it takes to make art and the importance of supporting the arts in the world, and she has never hesitated to support other artists' campaigns and efforts, especially if they use social media to build and reach their communities. However, the business as usual music companies and media companies cried foul with the Kickstarter campaign, and this just shows that we're in the midst of a massive transition phase in business and in life where exchange, value and ways of doing business are changing and sometimes conflicting.

For me, being able to share the many facets of your personality with others (like Amanda Palmer has done) was one of the reasons everything opened up for me. I was rewarded in social media for being my real self. I was rewarded by people listening to me, coming to my classes. Social media is about providing value. It's not about selling anymore. Selling doesn't work on social media. Adding value becomes the most important thing you can do. This can be making people laugh. It can be philosophical. It can be providing your product. It can be sharing pictures of bony sea creatures on the beach in Galveston with your dog like I did when I rented a house there for a month to work on this book!

Be your authentic self. (Get Real, People!). Listen to your heart with your intellect to guide you. Be purpose-FULL, and you can't go wrong! Note: If you don't know what your purpose is, no worries. It will come when timely. Each kernel in the bag of life pops when it should.

Let's see what our panelists had to say about our theme of "from business as usual to business as purpose:"

Our Funday Panelists Share on
From Business as Usual to
Business as Purpose

Our From Business as Usual to Business as Purpose Panelists

Rachel Parker | Strategic Communications Consultant

"I love this topic. I came from a corporate background. When I was in that environment, everything was about the next promotion, the next title, the next raise. Around the time I turned 40, I said, 'This is ridiculous. It is always the next thing, the next thing, the next thing.' That's when I started to think about becoming a business owner. I read a book by Simon Simek called *Start with Why*. In it, he talks about how, from a branding standpoint, we usually start with the what - what we are going to do? Then we move into the how, and then we move into the why. So we make computers and we start with, this is how we make them and then this is why we make them. He suggests that if you look at successful brands, they actually do it the other way around. For instance, Apple starts with the why.

If you start with your purpose, there is no competition because everybody has a different why. We have been marketed every which way with slick tactics. I can't even go to the bathroom in a restaurant without having an ad in front of me. We are over it! In my experience, getting over that perfect Photoshopped, capital 'P' professional version of yourself and just being honest and open helps you and your business live out your purpose."

Sharon Jenkins | Author, Editor, Ghostwriter

"One of the things that really rocks my world is the fact that we have gotten so into conforming to what industry says is 'the proper business posture' that we are trying to step into cookie cutter roles that don't fit. All that energy should be put instead into embracing who you are and going back to the master creator and figuring out, 'Hey! What did you design me to do?' I do business because I can't do anything else; it is my DNA to do business and to be a business owner. I was designed to be unique and purposeful, but I had to give myself permission to do that. And I believe that you really create a more positive atmosphere in the world when you decide that you are going to embrace your purpose. That's why business as usual should be business as purpose, because business as purpose is business on purpose."

J-Coby Wayne commented:

"Purpose doesn't always reveal itself quickly. Sometimes it takes an entire lifetime of searching for the purpose. A life is a path of searching for the purpose, so many people try many different things to get in touch with what their purpose really is. One of the things I always encourage people to do is just keep asking the question, 'What is my purpose?' It is guaranteed that you will get the answer eventually. That reward comes from the persistence of asking the question and exploring the question. Our purpose is hard-wired into who we are. I asked the question all my life, and I finally got the answer when I was 33 years old after experimenting with many different things."

Carra Riley | Realtor

"I just got back from traveling in the Baltic region where the average age of my fellow travelers was about 79. That got me thinking about what you really give to mankind, even if it is to just to one person. It is that love, that genuine concern and the passion for what you have to be able to share with someone else no matter what the business product or service is, to help others - that is business as purpose to me. Every business, product or service should be asking themselves before they start their marketing, before they start their content, 'What is my reason and purpose for being? Is it to impart truth, health and happiness?' Ask yourself what it is that you want to do, then follow that love."

Suzette Cotto | Innovate Social Media

"Thinking about making meaning versus making money for this topic, I was reminded of an interview I had back in 2005 with the comptroller of a company. I expected that he would want to know how I was going to bring something to the bottom line and what my value in dollars would be to the company. But instead, he asked me what kind of a legacy I planned to leave to the company. That was a really unexpected question for me, and I had to think of it in a much more thoughtful way than the usual dollars and cents kind of way. Leaving a legacy became something that I continued to think about with everything I did from that point on. It was important to me in business to make sure that I was creating quality relationships with quality people and populating quality energy around whatever project I was working on and whomever I was working with.

From that point on my business perspective became: Is this good for me? Is this good for my people? Is this good for my company? Is this good for my family? Does it honor God? If I can check off each one of those things, then I know I am leaving a legacy rather than just working in a job. My work became a mission as a person rather than as an employee doing a job."

J-Coby commented:

"I just wanted to acknowledge that comp-troller Suzette mentioned because corporate gets a lot of bum rap these days, but I think there have always been pockets of really enlightened people in business. I experienced a couple of interviewers like the comptroller as well, and I always appreciated the ones that surprised me. I always packaged myself so well for interviews, I loved it when somebody threw me a curve ball and really made me think. And I think that creating this capacity to think through mental challenges is the best of what enterprise and what business offers us when we get together in large groups."

J-Coby Wayne | Agent of Evolution

"This topic really gets to the heart of what I really love to do and what I think I am here to do. Part of what I am here to do is to create meaningful experiences. And meaning has always been where it is at for me. In talking about business as purpose, I want to start with an example of a company that starts with the why and starts with the purpose, GoPro. GoPro makes what

Wired magazine called 'a clunky little camera.' It started in 2004. It was just a surfer dude who was about 20 or something like that at the time. He was hanging out on his surfboard with his friends and wanted to have a way to capture their rides and share their surfing experiences and the waves.

The GoPro camera is not fancy, but they have done a lot of really cool stuff in finding ways to harness it to your body or your surfboard or your skateboard or your hang glider or your dog. Because of how they started out as a couple of guys just wanting to share their waves and because of listening to the users of their product, they have created a brand that is so powerful because when you see someone with a GoPro, you know they are going off and are about to do something awesome.

We've been driving all across the country since April, and all these motorcycle riders have these GoPros on their helmets as they are riding around. This is brilliant stealth guerilla advertising that wasn't even part of what GoPro set out to do. Brilliantly, they created a YouTube channel where GoPro users can share the videos shot with their GoPros. Some astounding number like 8.5 million hours of video have been posted in the last few years.

They've recently done a deal with Virgin Airways where Virgin flights will include the awesome adventures of GoPro videos posted by the users as part of their in-flight programming. This is a really good example of a company that is booming just by doing what they love - business as purpose. People told them that they were crazy, that they were not going to boom as a business based on the finite basic technology of little unsophis-ticated box cameras, but the market has proven the naysayers wrong, and GoPro went public in 2014.

At a more personal level, my experience in the work that I do is that we are all truly hardwired with a blueprint, and our job and opportunity in this life - whether personally or as participants in enterprises or communities or families or churches or whatever community - is to boldly have experiences that help us plug into the reality of that blueprint.

No matter what is happening in the environment, no matter what is happening in our lives, no matter whether an enterprise is 'up' or 'down,' reaching people, not reaching people, making money, not making money...none of that really matters as long as we stay focused on the why and the purpose and the meaning. Then we don't get lost in the thicket of daily happenings around us. When we are expressing our purpose, it is irresistible, and people get attracted to what it is that we are bringing to life."

Shelley commented:

"It is so true that people are so thirsty for realness, and when you are living your passion, when you are living what you are supposed to be doing, they want it, they are thirsty, and that is why I am successful. It is not because I know Facebook inside and out, which I do, or LinkedIn, which I do. It's because I'm authentic."

Suzette commented:

"People don't want to gravitate towards something that they know isn't going to be a positive energy in their life. If we show who we really are inside and within our universe, like J-Coby said, you are a magnet for positive energy."

Shelley" Thanks, panelists, for a very purposeful discussion!"

Shelley's Wrap-Up

PRACTICE

Here are six practical suggestions from Yellow Brick Road founder, Ian Hacon, on how to connect with your purpose. Specialized in management consulting, he says that finding your purpose (or reconnecting with it) will bring immediate benefits to your well-being and could extend your life. This has been demonstrated through a large study by University College London that was published in the respected health publication, *Lancet*. That study of 9,050 English people with an average age of 65 found that lifespan is substantially lengthened by having a sense of meaning and purpose. The people in the study who stated having a strong sense of meaning and purpose were 30% less likely to die over the study's eight-and-a-half year follow-up period than those with a lower sense of well-being derived from meaning and purpose

These are the steps Ian Hacon suggests you can try to explore to strike upon your purpose:

1. Write down what you care about in life. What's important to you? What are your values?

2. Think about where you want to go in life. Think about what you want your obituary to sound like, what's your legacy? Write this down.

3. Compare 1 and 2 above to where you are now. What are the big differences?

4. Think about what needs to change to get you on track with your purpose. Write it down and make an action plan for change.

5. Make a public declaration of your intent. This will get your emotional self more committed to not failing.

6. Get a coach. Have someone to challenge and support you on the journey. This could be a professional coach; it could be a friend.

Business as purpose isn't just some new age idea at the fringes anymore. It's not just entrepreneurs and solopreneurs who are focusing on purpose. More traditional businesses are starting to see the light. Just as we were finishing edits on the book, I found an amazing read in the *Huffington Post*. It shares how PricewaterhousesCoopers LLC (PWC), an auditing, tax and consulting juggernaut, is launching a new platform to spotlight "the ways businesses are working toward solutions and widening the lens of their concern in ways that benefit not only the bottom line, but also their employees, their communities and the world at large." According to the article, "Purpose + Profit will feature stories, insights and tips from leaders in the world of business and thinkers who are driving change, with an emphasis on what's working in entrepreneurship, B-corporations - that is, benefit corporations, a class of corporations that strive to have a positive impact on society - and impact investing." We've provided the link to the full article in the Resources appendix at the end of this book.

PricewaterhouseCoopers is the result of the merging of some of the biggest and oldest accounting, audit and consulting players in the world. When these "big guys" start coming to the purpose table, you know it's an idea that's starting to be taken seriously. Time will tell how - and how much - business as purpose will start to penetrate business as usual as a new business culture. One thing we can count on: If big business starts turning its creativity, resource-fulness, great minds, inventiveness, skill at strategic alliances, influence and money towards new ways of bringing business as purpose to life, it will be a beautiful new day and world!

C H A P T E R S I X

Principle #6:

From Profits to Principles

What does "success" look like in your business?

That's the question we asked our panelists to explore in our sixth hangout in the series, "From Profits to Principles." This topic made me reflect on all the times my principles were comprised by the over-emphasis on profits or the perceived need for profits! There were so many instances in my corporate life, as well as in my own business, where my intuition or gut told me, "NO"! And sometimes it was such a soft little "no" - not a BIG NO - that I shoved it down and didn't listen.

When I think of business as profit, I think of money and the traditional bottom line of a balance sheet with profits and losses. There's nothing wrong with profits. There's nothing wrong with being a business that's making a profit. But a business that only cares about profits and about none of the other conscious bottom-line is a business as only profit. A business as profit will do anything and everything without regard to employees, the environment, their community. If they're public, it's all about profit and dividends for the shareholders at the absolute extreme of a company running strictly for profit.

Many of these kinds of companies still do extremely well since much of the economic world structure is set up to run this way, but several very high-profile failures ultimately contributed to the 2008 world economic collapse that continues to send out ripples of consequences, including eroding the middle class: Enron (fraudulent concealment of large losses), Adelphia Communications (internal corruption with directors sentenced to prison), WorldCom (directors used fraudulent accounting practices to push stock prices up), Arthur Andersen (obstruction of justice through shredding documents related to the Enron collapse), Bear Stearns (over-investment in the sub-prime mortgage market), Lehman Brothers (heavy investment in mortgage debt and attributed as the direct creator of the 2008 economic collapse), AIG (over-investment in sub-prime mortgages), Refco (CEO concealed $430 million in bad debts), Bayou Hedge Fund Group (founder and hedge fund manager defrauded investors and orchestrated fake audits), Bernie Madoff's massive Ponzi scheme that bilked investors out of millions. (Please note: Many good and honest people worked for these companies, but the gaps in principled leadership created the conditions for these companies to fail and take many people down with them.) Companies where leadership has a very strong will with very high intelligence sometimes fall into the trap of their own cleverness and power, and the guiding conscience of the heart either isn't there in the first place or it falls by the wayside because there's a highly internally competitive culture that doesn't reward the executives or employees to "have a heart" or stand up for principles that may be different from the company line.

The incentive in a business as profit is the more profit you make, the more money you get. If you're a salesperson and you meet quota, you get X%. If you exceed quota, you get a bigger percentage or more travel (like all-expense-paid two weeks to

Tahiti) - but certainly not more time off! I never bought into these rewards even though I received many of them. For me, it was part of the game and the culture. I was great at wearing the mask, and it was almost like the universe gave me the top of the mountain right from the beginning. The first month I was a sales consultant, I made $15,000 in fees, but I never felt it was about closing the deal, even though I was pressured to do that. However, the part that felt purposeful even in the midst of this was being the farmer, nurturing, caring, heart-based. That was natural. That was purpose. I always felt great about building relationships.

All the time in corporate America, I went against my principles because I was paid to close deals. I always had a sense of dis-ease the whole 20 years I was in corporate sales. The effect was that I never allowed myself the space to listen. I had no confidence to believe in my intuition and my gut. Who was I to know anything? Power and money were where it was at.

I might have stayed in corporate forever for the almighty dollar if my internal guidance system hadn't kicked in, causing me to start questioning things and speaking my mind. My mind was starting to open because I was sick of feeling sick. I realized there had to be a better way. I wasn't fulfilled even though I was making money and was very successful. I was starting to take elective coursework that caused me to realize that there was a lot more to me than just closing deals. That opened my confidence in myself as a thoughtful human being with the right to be and grow. The result, as I've shared in other chapters, was getting fired, and getting fired gave me the space and time to explore what was next.

Learning to listen to your intuition, your heart, your higher self takes observation and repetition. It was easy for me to ignore my intuition and heart for a time, but it was definitely "dis-ease" to not listen. When I worked for big companies, they were paying me, so I thought I had to listen to what I was told to do, even though I knew it was wrong. I was trying to be something I wasn't and was acting and reacting in a way that didn't feel right. Yet I was programmed that it was the right way.

In contrast to business as profit, business as principle does things for the right reason. The right reason is something that you know in your heart and your gut - whether it's not agreeing to do something asked of you in a corporate setting or walking away from an opportunity or a partnership if you are a business owner or leader. Business as principle walks away from selling a solution that isn't the right fit. A business as principle does not hurt the environment or humanity. They do not pollute. They do not lie. They are not deceitful or deceptive, even if being deceitful would benefit their shareholders and profit. The goals and objectives of a business as principle reflect more than profitability.

Business as principle values and listens from its whole being and not just its intellect or power. A principled business - or a person or other entity - isn't self-absorbed. It isn't myopic. It is more concerned with growth and betterment and contributing beyond itself. A principled business values employees as individuals and parts of the whole. It invests both money and time in helping them grow and develop. A business as principle operates in the recognition and reality that abundance attracts abundance. When you invest in others, it will come back to you because of the Law of Attraction. The business reaps what it sows. Whether it's giving to the employees or the community, they are part of all that. It brings a harmonious environment.

Some 20 years on from my "dis-eased" career in corporate sales with business as profit, I thankfully have evolved, and I have trained my listening to "hear" when something is wrong. I know now (practice makes perfect!) that when the energy isn't there, when it doesn't feel right, DON'T DO IT! I get a lot of opportunities to speak, train and consult with businesses, but sometimes the alarms go off, and I do not feel in tune, energetically speaking, with that person or organization. It is inevitable that when I do NOT listen to this and proceed because the mighty greenback calls to me, and profits drive the decision, then, it is NOT the right decision.

An example Tom Ferguson gives in his book, *Peerless*, of a business operating from principle as well as profits is Sterling Bank. Sterling Bank is a local bank in Houston, and the founder, George Hernandez, was very, very clear from the outset that he was not going to follow the convention of sending out credit card applications to struggling college kids because he knew that hitting this demographic was just not the right way to go. College kids are the last group that needs to build debt and be paying twenty percent interest on that debt. So he defied convention and said, "We are not going to be a business that comes from decisions based solely on profits. We are a business based on principles."

Another example in Tom's book that spoke to me is Bridgeway Management, a mutual fund led by John Montgomery. Bridgeway is a very successful mutual fund company, based on the measure of profitability. Most companies basically take all their profits and pour them back into the company, especially in the early going. John did it differently with his company. He decided that they were going to take 50% of profits and put them into non-profits. This is a great example of a company doing social good. This approach totally went against convention, but he basically felt that this mode of operating accelerated Bridgeway's growth. According to John, had he never done this, they would have had half the growth that they have experienced to date. So being a generous company and contributing to social good makes good business sense.

Let's see what our panelists had to say about "from profits to principles:"

Our Funday Panelists Share on
From Profits to Principles

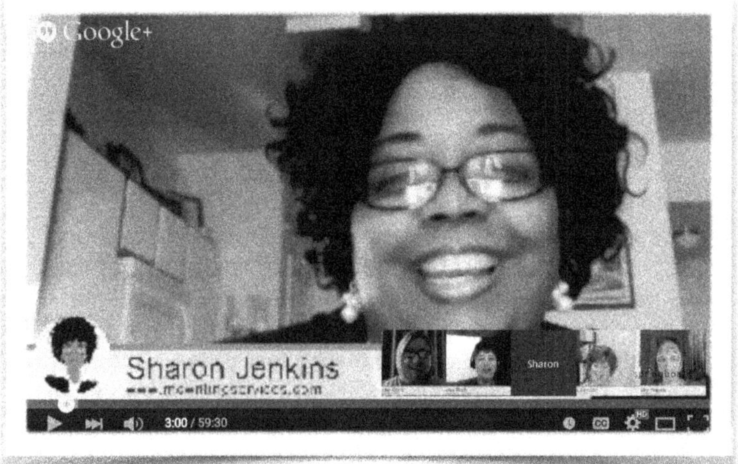

Our From Profits to Principles Panelists

Sharon Jenkins | Author, Editor, Ghostwriter

"This topic has made me reflect on who I am as a business owner, what motivates my moral core and how that influences other people. It makes me ask myself, 'How do I balance my social responsibilities with being a profit-generating business?' When you are trying to make a major transition that also means that your brand is changing in the process. I think that it all starts with you! What is your billboard, and how do you represent when it comes to your customers? What messages are you sending out?

To answer these questions, you really have to know what your moral core is and then establish your business around that. I don't know that you can concretely say, 'This is what I am going to do, this is what I am going to say' ahead of every moment because we live in an ever-changing environment. But one thing that I do know is that you can represent your core value system in your business. Based on all the women that I have seen on the panel today, we have a love for the world that we live in, and we are keenly responsible or have a sense or a responsibility for what we do in that environment, the world that we live in.

I am currently reading *The E-Myth Revisited*. I just want to read something to the listening audience, 'We often wonder, how do I get people to do what I want? How do I get people to follow me? How do I get people to have confidence in who I am and the product that I am delivering? How is it good for them?' The author says that this is the question that he hears most often, and the answer he gives is, 'You can't! You can't get your people to do anything! If you want to have it done, you are going to have to create an environment in which doing it is more important to your people than not doing it! And where doing it well becomes a way of life for them.' So the whole moral of this particular story is what image are you projecting, and is it an image that other people can really sense? Can they sense your compassion for society and your compassion for them? Are you showing them that you care? C-A-R-E in capital letters!"

Suzette Cotto commented:

"I think it is good to promote social consciousness with your business, but you also have to really be authentic about it or people will see right through it. It can undo your business if you pick some cause to support that isn't a fit for you or that you're clearly not passionate about."

Shelley commented:

"I absolutely agree with that statement! If you don't do it for the right reasons, you are not going to attract good back to you. You can just sniff out a rat, especially when you are in tune with the world of energy. I was already pretty in tune anyway because I have always been this authentic person, but after working with J-Coby and Kain over the years, I think I am even more aware now of what I attract and who I attract by who I am being, so I mirror and reflect what I want to come back to me."

Suzette Cotto | Innovate Social Media

"For this topic, I tried to think about my concept of where money comes from. And I think a lot of that is riddled by what money was to our parents. Growing up as a child in the 1960s and the beginnings of social responsibility where people were becoming more socially conscious played a big part in how I took attitudes towards money into my professional life. I am a happy person because I now own my own business where I get to call the shots.

If something isn't congruent with my values, I get to choose not to participate with that. My personal values are rooted in everything that I do. I just had a flash of a thought: What if customer, employee and community satisfaction could be included as part of the annual Profit & Loss Statement? Customer service should be part of the bottom line. It would be great if I could put together a high-tech report for everybody that shows a business cycle of corporate responsibility. This would build trust and relationships with clients. I think that is one reason I love social media so much. I get to build real relationships with the people that I work with and that I care about. I get to know that my clients know that I genuinely care about their business, their passion, why they exist.

If you are self-employed or a small business, you are putting your heart and soul into what you are doing. And people want to know that you value them. It is the same with customers, so the results of trust and engagement should be some pretty good sales. The whole point for this generation is not just how many people can you get likes from; it is how many people are following you because they have a congruent value system with you - what is important to them, is important to you and vise versa - so you have to stand for something in business these days. It is not good enough to say, 'I have this great widget for sale. Don't you want to buy it?' You have to attach something human to it or nobody wants it."

Lisa Boesen commented:

"Suzette resonated with me because I was reading a Tweet this morning about an article on how our perception of time affects how we value money, depending on whether our perception of money is in the past or in the future. Then I started connecting all my dots thinking about how I perceive time and finances and why I chose to have a small business even though in having a small business, you may not have a business plan or count your beans. But you are in business because you really want to cut your own cord and find out what your business is going to look like and how you are going to approach your customers, your products and your service. That's the whole integrity piece of it. It is hard for me, coming from my old HR perspective, not to think in terms of having a mission statement and having clarity on your core values and what drives you."

Lisa Boesen | Consultant, Speaker, Facilitator, Coach

"Money isn't everything, especially if a project or work doesn't seem right or doesn't feel right. For me, I won't take something on if it doesn't fit the three R's - right me, right place, right time. I had a company reach out to me, and the money was going to be really good. But I had to go through this panel interview with five people on the call, and it was as wrenching as a job interview. I really liked the content, but I couldn't figure out how it was going to go with their conference because it was a group of analysts and actuaries in healthcare. And it was on the provider side of health care involving insurance. They really wanted someone to come in and speak with passion, and I just couldn't figure out how to make it work between their questions and how I could deliver the content.

In hindsight, I am glad that I wasn't chosen. I have no idea who they finally went with or even if they rethought the whole thing. The money might sound really great, but if it is not your topic or it is not the right me, right place, right time, it is not a fit. Out of this type of experience, now when I talk to individuals, I am much more forthright. I tell them if I think am not the right person. I won't twist the topic to make myself fit. If you try to make a talk fit for the money, you could get up and totally bomb it."

Shelley commented:

"Lisa, you've reminded me that two days ago I was approached by the largest hospital organization in the Houston area to come in and present to the doctors and the researchers to train them on LinkedIn. And they started drilling me... Have you ever spoken to blah blah blah... My gut was screaming to me, 'This just doesn't feel right!' As much as I knew I could come in there and do what they wanted in my sleep, I knew that it wasn't right for me."

Suzette Cotto commented:

"Going back to being socially responsible and authentic, just this last week, I had an instance where I felt like the person that I was working with as my client was not being socially responsible. So we have it coming from all sides how and when we choose to do business with someone coming from a place of principles and not just profits. It is not just consumers we are interacting with who are being socially responsible or irresponsible, but also business associates, people that we do business with. Sometimes that puts me in a really hard position because, for instance, a business associate owes me money, and I have to walk away and say, 'I can't do this anymore and hope that this doesn't affect me and my reputation as a business.'"

J-Coby Wayne | Agent of Evolution

"I could talk about this topic of From Profits to Principles for years! The question of whom we partner with as clients or business associates or service providers or vendors so that we are staying within our principles is a really good question. The challenge in a lot of ways is, How do we know? How do we know if a client, business associate, service provider or vendor is totally aligned with our values and principles?

When we look into where to have our bank accounts, for example, not a lot of people consciously know that the bank where they put their money uses that money to invest in the stock market. If we have a bank account at a big bank, and we have a personal commitment to not investing with companies that invest in certain businesses like tobacco, alcohol, soda, processed food, guns, gambling, we have no control over our money being put into those stocks that we want nothing to do with for reasons of principles. The only way we have any control over this is by not putting our money into a big bank account, but it might not be practical NOT to bank with a big bank.

The tentacles of business are so positively and not-positively infused and engrained into society that even when we want to make conscious choices to work with certain companies or not work with them, we are touched by these tentacles, whether we like it or not. This gets at one of the underlying things that we haven't really discussed yet, and that is part of the reason that we are even having this discussion of profits to principles. In pretty much all of current life and in for-profit business (especially publicly-traded companies), the only currency that is really measured and valued is profitability.

Where this gets interesting is that publicly-traded companies have an incredible capacity to do good. The whole concept of the stock exchange is that it is meant to create a public exchange where the public has the opportunity to benefit from the growth of a company. And a company gets fueled to grow through the participation of the public, not just by the people who are working within the company as employees. So it is very interesting and skewing and distorting in this day and age that the only currency, pretty much the only way by which a company is measured in terms of success in the public sphere as well as in the business sphere, is profitability.

On the other hand, there are non-publicly-traded companies that have managed to come from principles as well as profit. REI, the outdoor gear and adventure store, is a great example. They are a co-op. They have not had to go public, and they have been able to continue to grow by being a privately-owned and customer-owned company. Another good example is Wheatsville Co-op in Austin, Texas, a grocery store that features many locally-grown and healthy food options. It is interesting that a lot of people and businesses believe that in order to be able to stick to their principles, they have to stay private and can't go public. By law, going public changes the yardstick by which companies become measured - creating profitability for shareholders.

So a big part of the conversation around this topic is considering what currencies are in business. REI considers one of its major currencies to be stewardship of the environment. Their slogan is, 'At REI we inspire, educate, and outfit for outdoor adventure and stewardship.' They have invested millions and millions of dollars into helping to steward the environment. They started with principles that have enabled them to stick to who they are.

Going a layer deeper to the world of energy, there are three essential components or principles that underlie any system that functions successfully - whether it is a human being or a pine cone or an ecosystem or a city. These are also three principles that are needed for a fully functioning enterprise. These three are: 1) the will principle, or the spark or principles or vision or purpose of an idea 2) the love-wisdom principle, which is the glue and essentially the human relations in an enterprise, the piece that binds everything together to make sure that the principles are being put into practice and 3) the mind principle, the creative intelligence and the execution of the ideas. That is the basic triangle needed in any functioning organization or enterprise. If any one of those pieces is off or isn't present, then the enterprise becomes 'sick.'

For instance, in the case of AIG, the majority of people there were probably good. But AIG got really trapped by investment banking companies that started to play a game with insurance. Morgan Stanley and other companies started to bet against the very products that they were selling, knowing that they would go out of business. But in the process, the top executive at AIG walked away with millions upon millions of dollars to the power of three. The leaders of the investment banks and the insurance com-panies like AIG knew that the practices that they were doing would run their own companies into the ground, and it didn't matter because they knew that they would walk away personally with millions. That is so completely skewed!

Referring to our three principles, there was clearly a lot of will (power and drive to generate and wield lots of money) and clearly a lot of clever intelligence (to figure out how to manipulate insurance money), but the love-wisdom was lacking. If there is love-wisdom in the leadership of an organization, the leaders don't - in fact, can't - do things that harm their employees, their customers and the economy for their personal gain because the conscience of the heart makes it contrary to their very DNA to violate principles of goodwill, truth and stewardship.

Everything in business, everything in nature, starts with an idea, and that idea can be ill-intended or well-intended, or the idea can be neutral. Basically how we put it into motion and the principles that we use to share the ideas or commercialize the ideas, to spread the idea, to make the idea public, is when value judgment comes in regarding whether something is positive or negative, evolutionary or involutionary.

If the heart isn't there to accompany and regulate the will and the mind through its function as a holder of the principles, the conscience and the positive enforcement that lets the ideas continue to flow in a positive direction, you lose your ethics.

The last thing I want to talk about is the way money is designed to work. When you think of money as energy, it is essentially a by-product of a good idea shared with good principles. A lot of the tensions that we are seeing in the world and in business today around seemingly bad people doing bad things with money are designed to get the public and business leaders starting to see that profit is not the only measure. It is a good measure, it is a very concrete neutral measure in a way, but it can start to be accompanied by bad things happening to give us a chance to come up with creative solutions.

The more evolved you become, the more your focus becomes bringing good to the world, and enterprises are really set up to do that. We often forget that because businesses often get such a bad rap. But corporations, if they are built and running according to principle, are really community drivers. They are meant to create value and plenty for many, many, many people and communities. Business is an incredible force of good and principles in the world. A lot of the employees who lost everything at Enron and AIG are being pressed to become resourceful in new ways, and a lot of them have succeeded."

Shelley: "Thank you, panelists, for your wise words!"

Shelley's Wrap-Up

It's been my and the panelists' experience that your principles will drive your profits. And profits and other assets can be measured in many different ways beyond money. (We'll explore this more deeply in Chapter 9.) Do what you love lovingly and with principles, love what you do, and the profits will follow!

CHAPTER SEVEN

Principle #7:

From Productivity (Doing) to Presence (Being)

This topic was originally "From Human Doings to Human Beings", however, I wanted to put the old corporate angle on it so we could talk about being present when doing production!

What happens in my life is I get so busy, and I forget that being present in my doing is what is important. I think that when I am "in the flow" and am creating work from my being, I am at my best. This is what I want, not "having to" do something like write a curriculum or create a presentation or a video for my newsletter. I am being present when I come from "WANT TO" versus "HAVE TO" and when I am not coming from a place of lack. The energy that flows from wanting to do something versus having to is a positive, vibrant energy compared to the negative, uncomfortable "have-to" space.

VARIOUS VOICES SPEAK ON BEING PRESENT

"

Being Present is what we experience when we are completely at peace with this very moment. It is a life journey where we constantly grow our inner peace... Being present is a time frame you choose to focus on... The path to being more real in the present is to stop comparing... Being present means learning to live as if we have nothing to hide, nothing to prove and nothing to lose... The simplest way to master being present is to practice The First Rule of Inner Peace. The first stage is to gain control over our racing mind. The second stage is to gain control over our volatile emotions. The third stage is to connect deeply with our soul. Being neutral and non-judgmental before taking action is the key to being present, positive and at peace. When we are being present, we are tuned in to our 'Quiet Inner Voice.' This is sacred.

"

- John Kuypers
personal leadership coach-author-speaker

---

5 STEPS FOR BEING PRESENT

1. ***Take a breath.***
Breath, along with change, is the only constant.

2. *Ask and consider the question,* ***what am I doing right now?***

3. ***Be a witness.***
In any given moment, observe it, name it and stand away from it.

4. ***Let the rest go.***
Many people think nirvana means bliss or peace, but it actually means "no holding" or "no clinging." Travel light - what we do not need in that moment, don't take on board.

5. ***Come back to the breath.***
When the world or your thoughts begin to again intrude, simply come back to the breath.

- Michael J. Formica, MS, MA, Ed.M.
psychotherapist, teacher and writer

---

7 LIFE LEARNINGS FROM 7 YEARS ON "PRESENCE"

1.
Allow yourself the uncomfortable luxury of changing your mind.

2.
Do nothing out of guilt, or for prestige or status or money or approval alone.

3.
Be generous with your time and your resources and with giving credit and, especially, with your words.

4.
When people try to tell you who you are, don't believe them.

5.
Build pockets of stillness into your life.

6.
Presence is far more intricate and rewarding an art than productivity.

7.
Debbie Millman says, "Expect anything worthwhile to take a long time."

- Maria Popova
Founder and Curator of *Brain Pickings*

Business is so focused on profit as the only measure of success. Our topic in this Funday is a reminder that what matters most is really not what we do, but who we are being when we do it! We have an amazing opportunity to be present in all that we do, and not be thinking about what we "should" be doing or what happened yesterday or where we need to be in one hour. We can focus on the present, as a present, and be accepting or forgiving or in the moment and just be your true authentic self. We as humans want to be heard, accepted and loved. You have to be present to be doing the right things.

After working in corporate America for so many years, I lost sight of being present. When we were kids, we just were. We didn't worry about tomorrow or even the next minute. We were in the moment. I am not saying that my work isn't important. I love what I do in social media, but who I am BEING when I am doing that work is what has become so much more important than the work itself. Am I truly listening when someone asks me a question? Am I present? Am I focused on them? Am I committed to the individual and their uniqueness?

Sometimes a life crisis like 9/11 occurs, and it is a huge wake-up call for a lot of people to question, "What am I doing? Why am I doing this? Am I happy? Is this feeding my soul? Is this my purpose in life?" Sometimes something has to occur to slap us upside the head and get us back on track. When we are really in our element, when we are present, it is natural, it is who we are. In my first book, *Get Real, People!*, which is about being your authentic self in social media, it was about just being real. When you have to think about who you are being, or create an avatar of who you want to be, you are not entirely being your authentic self.

How many years I invested in doing the things required to be the best salesperson! Now don't get me wrong: Those years weren't wasted. We have to learn from our experiences so the next iteration of where we are to go will appear. Who I am today is based on all the "Miss Takes" I made along the way.

Like most people, I struggled for so many years, asking, "What do I want to be when I grow up?" Sometimes it is difficult to know that because our culture is all about saying, "What do you want to do when you grow up?" The question should be, Who do you want to be when you grow up? Ask yourself, "Who am I?" Ask yourself what qualities you want to bring to your experience of living every day.

Whether it is writing or dancing or training like I do, if you are stuck, help yourself shift out of stuckness by asking yourself what you want to bring to life. Which of your qualities were you born with that you want to share? What is it that flows for you without excessive thought and effort? What is it that flows so joyfully that time seems to fall away, and you don't think of it as work? Consider these questions, and then match your talents to what you want to be able to do out there in the world. It takes a lot of thought and practice to be present, so make sure to let yourself sit down and be still and think about the question of "Who am I?"

Honestly, I've struggled with this question for years. When I was a teacher way back in the day teaching fifth grade, I didn't appreciate the innate teacher in me. I didn't know this was my gift, this is who I am as a human being. Then after my years of suffering in corporate, it hit me that I wanted to get back to my roots, I wanted to teach. And I wanted to combine my passion for business with my love of teaching, and boom! I created social media coursework for business, and voila, I was a teacher again. I love teaching, that is who I am. That is my gift, my passion and my purpose. I don't try to pretend to be someone I am not when I am teaching. I am totally present to my purpose, and the great thing now is that the material I will be presenting from this book takes me to the next level of instilling good in the world through teaching! Bringing conscious business principles and practices to people is even more rewarding for me than teaching social media!

So I am trying to learn, or re-learn, at all times that in the end what really matters to me is not my ability to produce a great social media course (although that is important). What truly matters is delivering that work and BEING present, loving, kind, accepting and a great listener through the delivery.

My years as a student and later as a teacher and assistant principal in public school education were as valuable as my corporate years in learning how **not** to do things! The world of education isn't immune to the "doing disease." In fact, it's probably a large contributor to a business culture of over-valuing doing as compared to being. When teachers have to "teach to the test" like the TAKS in Texas, the human element gets lost. The individuality gets lost. It was already happening back in my day, but it's worse today. It's trying to put a square peg in a round hole and make everyone conform.

As a student, I was always that square peg myself. I never did well with grades, but schools measure you by grades the way companies measure you by profit. It's very short-sighted. I remember being a child in school having a spark for art in the eighth grade. I remember drawing a self-portrait. I was so proud of what I did. I got encouraged by the art teacher. But somebody else squelched that, and my grades weren't good, so any spark of creativity that I had when I was in school got snuffed out. It was all about learning. There was no room for creativity. It was all black and white.

I remember teachers always saying to me that I could do the hard things, but I couldn't do the easy things. I grew up thinking I was stupid because I didn't test well. It took me till I was 40 years old and getting fired to embrace my "stupidity" as a gift. I may have been stupid in book learning, but man, did I have common sense and relatability! In a perfect world - in a school as purpose - there would be recognition and measurement of other gifts - whether artistic ability or relatability - and not just productivity. What do we do with schools today? Practically every kid I know is on some ADD drug.

We're just drugging square-peg kids who are naturally creative, physical, outspoken... Just drug 'em up! We should embrace them, but that takes more individual attention, more money, more investment, and it certainly doesn't fit current trends of teaching to the test.

As a teacher and assistant principal, I was always a non-conformist, so the seeds of free-thinking that got me fired from corporate life were there early on! I remember wanting to be called Ms. instead of Miss. There was one Mormon parent who refused to let her daughter call me Ms. I also worked with gifted students when I first started, and talk about non-conformists! I launched the first gifted program in Pennsylvania, and that group of students was crazy - brilliant crazy! I loved those kids, but they were a handful and a half. I was the guidance counselor for the district, too. Their attention span was so short because they got bored quickly since they were so smart. They had off-the-charts IQ measurements and were given creative activities to release their brilliance. They weren't put in a box. The classes weren't from a textbook. They were creative. That was really fun. I'm sure I created some really cool curriculum for them.

But they were not well-adjusted out of the classroom. In the majority of cases, they had a hard time socially - another skill lacking in education. They were very spoiled. Their parents catered to their unique intellects. In most cases, they weren't very disciplined. I suspect many of them became the less-than-principled leaders of the types of businesses that we mentioned in the previous chapter that contributed to world economic recession due to lack of principles. These brilliant leaders often lead from an over-inflated ego, an over-active mind, an upbringing of entitlement, a lack of impulse to "play nicely with others" and a God complex that leads them to believe that they can do no wrong. It is said that Jeff Skilling of Enron was notorious for this kind of behavior that led the company down the path of ruin and the total destruction of the employees' retirement accounts.

Like the high-achievement, productivity-oriented smart kids in school who get different curricula and don't always have to play by the same rules as the "regular kids," high achievers in sales or software development are the ones who are rewarded for behaviors that are not always "grow-grow." The very smart developers that came up with the most solid code at the company I worked at were the ones who were given the same kind of rewards as the sales stars, just like in school. I think that reflected in every department - R&D, Admin, etc. I was never in a department or group that was incented or rewarded to act as a think tank. I would have loved that. I would guess maybe think-tank culture and brainstorming happened more in management or marketing. But the profit centers in companies are the ones that get all the money, kudos, rewards because the "value" and "productivity" of their contributions can be measured most easily. If you are working in a company as a SUPPORT to those profit centers, you are not usually as valued as the profit centers themselves.

It's interesting and ironic that when I first landed in sales at a *Fortune* 500 company, it was run by a bean counter. It was more of a family and much more laid-back because sales wasn't king. It was a stable, nurturing company. It was about maintaining longer-term relationships. They valued that. I was there for 15 years. I felt pressure, but never the kind of pressure I felt at a sales-led company. When I worked in sales at a company run by a sales guy, sales (and sales as the measure of productivity) was king. It was a pressure cooker where every department that wasn't a profit center was at our beck and call. That power and prestige of being part of valued "producers" also felt good to my sales shark self.

In my experience over the last 20 years working with small businesses, the company culture is more like a family environment. That's not to say that some of these businesses aren't all about the profits and the weekly sales meeting and that you don't have numbers to make. Some of these businesses do sell just to sell.

I hear in workshops a lot from my small-business participants, what's the ROI of social media? These people who are coming from a more traditional productivity mindset don't yet understand the principle of "give to grow." They don't understand it's not about them; it's what's in it for the recipient. That traditional mold of sell, sell, sell, that's a hard one to break for most salespeople on social media. They have to give it up. If you do the right thing, if you listen, if you support your clients and community, if you give them valuable content, you will never have to sell anything ever again, and the definitions and modes of how you are being "productive" change completely. Social media has opened up this whole world of equality where the little guy can outshine the big guy with all the bucks all day long. It's a beautiful world where not just the big budgets can buy the market. But it only works if you're real. You've got to be authentic. You've got to add value and give to grow.

You can measure your return on influence and your productivity by seeing if your likes on Facebook increase, if your connections and comments on LinkedIn increase, if people are joining your mailing list, if people are sharing and forwarding your posts, if your phone is ringing and people are seeking you out, if you're considered a thought leader. All of these might not be measured with a dollar sign. I've never had to concern myself with income since I started to work with social media and coming from giving to grow. It's the energy you put out. It's the Law of Reciprocity. Ultimately, our businesses run on money. That's a good thing. But it doesn't have to be all about money. I did a barter for a dental implant. I've done a barter for massages with a massage therapist. You can get paid with time at a client's vacation house - whatever you deem valuable.

Productivity in this social media world is about engagement. Are you engaging with your audience? Are you supporting them? Are you there when they need you? Are you answering their questions? The sales and the money become a by-product of doing all those other things.

What are some of the ways I am there when people need me? My Facebook page is a support page, not a sales or self-promotion page. Anyone can ask me a social media question on my business page, and I will answer it. You begin to build trust with people by letting them know you'll be there to answer their questions. Sending out a newsletter video tip every week builds my brand. Using that same video tip information to publish social media knowledge on LinkedIn broadens the community I'm reaching.

Social media has made it so easy for us to build our brands and credibility and, thus, build our productivity. Anyone can publish on LinkedIn and be searched by the LinkedIn community for their published work. That's a phenomenal way to connect with people and build trust.

What does productivity look like when you are being a human being as compared to a human doing, when you are in a space of presence? I'm being productive right now as I write this, looking at birds. Still, I immediately and automatically think that productivity equals money when I turn to considering productivity, but productivity can be more time and more time doing what you love. It's more than what you contribute to the balance sheet. It can be in quiet, in stillness, in nature. And productivity can be in accepting the energy that's readily available from all forms of life on the planet. That's my favorite form of productivity - just to be with nature. I spent too many years thinking doing nothing was being lazy. Now I realize doing nothing is productive and necessary for my being.

The human doing version of productivity is what we learned in school. We learned that we had to get A's on our report card.

In sales, we learned we had to make X dollars each year. That was productive.

But what about in other cultures? Other cultures might value sitting on the beach and staring out as productive. Other cultures value giving all employees the entire month of August off. Other cultures take siestas. Other cultures give fathers as well as mothers paid maternity leave. They don't see any of this time as wasted. They see happier, healthier, more balanced employees.

Over the years, I put so much pressure on myself thinking if I wasn't being productive - i.e., making money or finding ways to make money - then I was just wasting time. It's interesting to wonder how much more space I may have opened up to do something like discover the cure for cancer if I had understood and valued presence early on in my life and career. Being present can be productive. But what we think it means to be productive goes all the way back to what we're taught is valuable in kindergarten, including coloring inside the lines.

For many people, when we are being busy doing, we aren't present. We lose the present moment. We're usually thinking ahead or behind when we're doing. When I'm in the flow, I'm doing and that's okay. When people are doing, they have some kind of objective outside themselves that they're trying to accomplish. When I'm in the doing mode, I'm usually not conscious of my surroundings. I'm in my head; I'm not in my body. For me, that's imbalanced. If you're constantly worrying about doing, you're not feeding your soul. You're not giving yourself the opportunity to expand because there's no space there. Sometimes you just have to stop to let new stuff in.

If you don't do this, productivity comes to an abrupt halt. It's similar to diversity and its impact on productivity: If you only hire Caucasians aged 22-30 and don't let other demographics in, you'll ultimately grind to a halt because you become imbalanced and stale. You need to bring in other perspectives.

When you don't create space to be, you also tend to get self-focused and stifle awareness of your environment and others who can stimulate your creativity, connecting the dots in new ways and with fresh thinking. I remember when I used to go to networking meetings and supposedly be in conversations with someone, instead of being intently present and focused on them, I would be looking around the room seeing who was a better investment of my time. It's also happened back to me where someone who's talking to me is looking everywhere else for the more valuable person they should talk to. (There's Newton's principle again: for every action - my not listening - there is an equal and opposite reaction - someone not listening to me!) Even today when I'm talking to someone in one of my classes, 90% of the time I'm incredibly focused on one person, but every once in a while I get distracted, thinking about needing to cover more materials, and that's not good.

Taking time for pause and reflection expands your growth. We had a library at one of the *Fortune* 500 companies where we could supposedly go just to think and reflect, but no one ever used it because the actual culture was that we weren't being paid to think. I still need to remind myself to be and not do. When we work for someone - even ourselves - we may be so busy doing that we can forget to just be and let new energy and new thought come in.

When you let the presence switch be on, I find you have a lot more patience with people. You have a more caring attitude. You truly become a better listener. You're in the moment. You're not thinking about what you have to get done. You're not thinking about paying your bills. You're not thinking about the work you have to do. It's a gift because it allows you to let other people's energy enter yours, and an exchange happens. This is really being in the flow. I've been amazed to discover that when this becomes the new normal, things just happen without having to push so hard.

Let's see what our panelists had to say about "from productivity to presence:"

Our Funday Panelists Share on
From Productivity to Presence

Our From Productivity to Presence Panelists

Shari Joyce | Divine Consultant, Founder, Chief Spiritual Officer

"I am really going to pay attention to this theme of being compared to doing with my grandchildren. I have six grandchildren, and everything is about what do you want to be, what do you want to do? Does anyone ever say, 'I want to be me?' I would like to encourage that in them.

I do things, but that is not who I am. This took me many years of my life to understand and also to live by. To not equate my self-worth with how well I do things in life was a concept that took me many years to learn, and I tend to gravitate now towards partnerships with people who are in life transitions, assisting them with recognizing this in themselves as well.

You know there is a belief that permeates our culture and business and personal endeavors, and that says, 'If I am not always busy, then I am not accomplishing anything and I don't feel valuable.' I say that your work is not related to being too busy, too stressed and having a maximized schedule. I think we are doing this to kids right now. I mean, people consider that if they are not in volleyball, cheer squad, you know a million different lessons, then it is not okay.

I think that our self-worth and our value comes from within and that no matter how much we produce or get done in a day, we are still valuable. From a business standpoint, this could sound airy-fairy, but I don't think that it is. I think we truly have to have more invested in our own life than in any company that we might work for. Nobody is likely to tell you this of course - it's not really seen as the western thing to do - but I think if you don't take charge of your own life and spend some more time being and less time doing, then how do you know you are going in the right direction?

I had a wonderful opportunity to go to Peru where I volunteered in a home with 55 disabled children. When I got there, I was like, 'Really, God? Is this what you really want me to do?' What I found out was that my job there was to be love. From nine to eleven in the morning, I held infants that had cleft pallets, were missing a limb, etc. All I had to do for them was to be love. We did that again during the middle of the day with older children. This really helped me see that being love was one of the most important things that you can do, be.

I think that if you never take stock in sitting still and listening to that intuition within, then how are you ever going to know really who you are and what will bring you happiness and fulfillment? Maybe spending more time being, you'll become happier and more fulfilled. I say to those who are listening, at some point over the weekend, why don't you treat yourself to a bit more being and a bit less doing, and set aside some time to be quiet somewhere - maybe sitting outside, maybe looking at a lighted candle, whatever you need, whatever your inspiration is. Grab a pen and paper. Your mind is probably going to start to run, you are going to get this commentary, 'I got to do this, I got to do that,' all the things you have to do and all the things you have programmed for so long. Take that pen and paper, and write it all down to stop that chatter from going on in your head by capturing everything in writing so you no longer feel that you have to remember all of it. After that, you can let go, and you can be. When the to-do list has been written down, and the chatter has stopped and you have calmed down, you can be attentive to what bubbles up inside of you and to that still, small voice inside of you. I think by doing this, you will get a great message at your very core, the authentic you, who is really calling you towards a life of happiness and fulfillment."

Questions and comments from the audience:

From Griswold:

"How do you figure out how to be if you don't recognize what you are meant to be? If you start by being what you are and you do what that dictates and you have what that earns, where does growth come from? Do we grow into being what we are not yet?"

From Suzette:

"I think people get stuck with the how: How do I stop doing and start being? I am married to the having, and I know the shift is happening for so many people."

J-Coby Wayne commented:

"A really great way to start thinking about being is to think about the qualities you want to bring to any environment. You may have your job description, and this is necessary. It is important to recognize that we still need organization and structure, and we still need to do, but it is the question of *how* we are doing. If we are doing by being, then everything flows a little more naturally.

There are a couple of ways that we can start looking at being and defining 'who we be' and 'not who we do' or 'how we do.' We can look at one of the key aspects of role-playing games to get at one of the ways. In the pre-digital age, it was Dungeons and Dragons, and then we started to have the adventure games on Atari, and then we had the sophisticated online World of Warcraft. In all of these games, you have to choose to be an avatar. You choose a character, and the character we choose tells us a lot about who we believe ourselves to be or who we aspire to be.

One of the most influential moments I had along my path of trying to move from doing to being came while I was watching one of the *Lord of the Rings* movies. I had always seen myself as Frodo. Frodo is the one who is always questing after the rings, and I saw myself as the adventurous quester. But I realized about halfway through the movie that I am actually more like Samwise Gamgee. Samwise goes along with Frodo on all the adventures. He's the loving, not-very-cool helper, and he is - in the old medieval sense of the word - Frodo's 'help meet'. Frodo would not be able to do any of his questing without Samwise Gamgee there - helping, sacrificing, taking the hit for Frodo, distracting something in the path so that Frodo could go and do his thing. And I realized I have spent my whole life thinking and being told I was Frodo when I am actually a lot more Samwise Gamgee. I am often at my best as a help meet (though I do love to quest, so I need to be helping on a quest). I am here to support other people to succeed, and I have become wildly more successful at what I do when I realized that what I am really good at, what I love to be, is a helper, a supporter, a catalyst, a spark.

So this is one of the ways creatively for those who are on the call to start exploring and discovering 'who you be.' Start thinking about what character you would be from *Star Wars*. Not everyone is the Jedi Knight. What would you be in whatever story or fairytale? What character do you resonate with? Then take a look at what you would describe yourself as if you work for corporate. Say you are an accountant, and your title is accountant. But within your organization, what are you bringing as an accountant? Are you bringing adventure? Are you the listener? Are you the problem-solver? Are you the person that cleans up messes? If you start thinking about the qualities you bring, that is how you can start connecting with 'who you be' and not only what you do."

Sharon Jenkins | Author, Editor, Ghostwriter

"I am going to go personal and then I am going to go professional on this topic. I remember when I was about to get a divorce from my first husband, he said that I didn't know how to live life. Well, that was because I was stuck in the doing - doing the wife thing and doing the mother thing and doing the professional thing, and I was stuck! I was doing all that because someone had told me that that was what I needed to do. And so I lost me, I couldn't find me. One of the beauties of now being of age and having lived a little is that I can embrace the human condition.

If I do not know who I am, and I am stuck in the doing mode, I can't move forward into fulfilling my life's purpose. I am just a robot. I am being what other people want me to be instead of being whom I have been heavenly designed to be and fulfilling my life's purpose on the Earth. So one of the things that I want us to think about is that when foreigners come over to this country, the first question that we ask them is, 'What do you do?' We don't ask them, 'Who you be?' (laughter from the panelists...) We ask them what do you do? Part of the reason we do that is we have been socialized into that corporate mentality. I think it is an advantageous situation for an employer to brainwash you into thinking that what you do is more important than who you are. Because if you seek and search for who you are that may just take you out of the position that they have put you in, and you grow and you become something different, but they might not realize you can be a benefit to them as a result of your growing into something different.

When I found the courage to be who I am, it made a world of difference. Certain things started attracting themselves to me, things that fulfilled my purpose, things that made me grow up in certain areas of my life. Can you imagine being in your 50s and not walking in the fullness of who you are? I think that when we all find that "who-we-should-be," it contributes to having a harmonious world, a harmonious nation, a harmonious community, so I am in the mindset that I am encouraging children, first and foremost my children, to be what they are designed to be, and not make them conform to a corporate mentality or to what a greed mentality says that you need to do. You just become part of the machinery that makes or builds that particular mindset when you are a doer, when you are a robot, performing. I like being on the 'being' side a lot better than on the 'doing' side, and I have so much more wealth, self wealth, as a result. And I bring that to others as a result."

Janet Cohen commented:

"I believe that there is a real question about the corporate agreement in our country about what we are supposed to do and how we are supposed to be. We live in a society that says that you have to do a particular thing so that you will get your stuff and then you will be happy. Get it-do-have-be! The agreement is that if you do something, you will make money, and if you make money, you will get stuff, and if you have stuff, you will be happy. People like me don't fit into that mold. I believe that the way that the world is changing now is that it doesn't start with the corner that says do; it starts with the corner that says be.

If you are naturally who you were meant to be, according to God or the universe or the Goddess or whatever you believe in, if you be exactly who you are, what you do will be a natural outflow of who you are, and the universe will reward us for being authentic, and as a result of that, we can have stuff if we want it.

We can buy Shelley's new book, for example. So what we need to think about in our consciousness is shifting that 'do, have, be' to 'be, do, and then have.' Because the have is really optional, isn't it? We are living in a society where a lot of people are paying attention to the environment, and reusing, and recycling and repurposing and all of that.

The last thing I have to share for now is that I will never forget the first time I went to Los Angeles on a vacation. I was visiting with friends who lived there from Houston, Texas, and I remember meeting people from LA and being shocked because rather than asking the usual question of 'What do you do?,' they asked, 'How do you play?' At that point in my life, I was a grown-up, I was working really hard on my career, and I had totally forgotten what play was about. In LA, it was a cultural thing to focus on how you play - *Where is the beach? We are hanging out and working on our suntan. We are playing volleyball.* I thought that was a great way to create conversation."

Shelley commented:

"The bottom line is, we are all just molecules flying all over the place, so we might as well be having fun doing it!"

Ronda Suder | Filmmaker, Writer, Actress, Entrepreneur

"I remember in college, my mom kept asking me, 'Well, don't you want to know what you want to do?' For the life of me, I did not know what to specialize in or what degree to go into. I went into college with a whole semester under my belt. I could have graduated early, but I was like, 'How am I supposed to know what I want to do for the rest of my life? It just doesn't make a whole lot of sense to me.'

After graduating from school, I went through my corporate years and eventually realized something wasn't working, and I needed to transition out. I needed to transition to a 'being' place. I was working with a coach at the time, and she encouraged me to write a vision for my life. When I did this, I realized the qualities I wanted in my life. I knew what I wanted to feel in my life. I knew the type of people I wanted to be around, and so I started with that. I didn't know what I really wanted to do, but storytelling was a passion. Acting, writing, they come naturally and easily to me. I still didn't know what form the vision and skills would take on, but I knew how I wanted to be, how I wanted to show up and who I wanted to be around to do that. So that is one way to maybe try and figure out that being.

For me, it was getting really clear on how I wanted to show up. In my current work with my team at the credit union, we just did a behavioral analysis. Like J-Coby said, each person in their role (like accountant) was asked, 'What do you bring? What are the qualities?' The options were doer, talker, and supporter. I was very close to talker and supporter. I bring these qualities to whatever I am doing.

From a business perspective, I find that we get so focused on the doing or the 'how to' and the 'when to,' or we get so focused on the to-do list or the doing part of it, that when we are not in that space of being present, we may be missing opportunities that are coming through. If we have a road map, it is great to follow that road map, but maybe at some intersection, we need to go in a different direction. If we are in a space of presence or being, then we are open to receiving that information and being able to go in that different direction, which may create more efficiency and a better outcome.

I do think it is important sometimes to acquire the tools we need when we are in that doing space, but I know if I go there too much, I can tell because my body feels it, knows it. I start to feel a little stressed, I need to shift here and here and always step back, take a breath, and walk away. And then be okay with that and come back.

The other thing I wanted to share was I had a friend who told me, 'I just don't think I am being very productive when I am not making money.' And then she said something like, 'If I am not making money based on what I am enjoying, then I am not being very productive.' I told her, 'Then you are probably talking to one of the most unproductive people you have ever met.' As you are growing a business, you put a lot into it, and you are not always making money. Fortunately, I had another friend who said that some of the most productive work you will ever do is sitting on a rock."

Comment from Suzette in the audience:

"There is exponential value in finding thought leaders and groups such as this discussion group that emulate the who and the what you want to be. It is so hard to do anything by yourself."

Janet Cohen | Certified Life Coach

"Throughout this whole discussion, I have been thinking about the whole Zen of it all - you know - what do we be?, and what do we do?, and I was thinking about the grand teacher, Alan Watts, the man well-known for bringing Eastern thought to Western civilization. He's a very funny guy. You can watch him on YouTube. I remember hearing him say that the most important question that we can ever ask ourselves in our lifetime is: 'Who am I?' As he worked on that and thought about that, studied that, and meditated on that, the best answer that he could come up with was, 'Molecules in a bag of skin.'

As a coach who works with writers, and as someone who believes a lot in Zen Buddhism and practices some of it, I think about what is on the surface and what is on the underbelly. I would encourage you if you are really struggling with, 'Who am I?' and 'How do I get there?' and 'What do I do?' and all of that to take a piece of paper and at the top of the paper, write 'I am...' Then make an agreement with yourself that you are just going to free-flow consciousness. You are not going to think about it. Then write it down, you are not going to censor it, or erase it. You are just going to keep writing, 'I am, I am, I am, I am...' Give yourself five minutes, which will feel like an eternity. If you are an experienced writer, give yourself 20 minutes. 'I am...' When you finish that project, I want you to go to the Zen side of the underbelly and put 'I am not...', and do the same thing another five minutes or 20 minutes or whatever time you want. Smart phones are great; you can set the timer and just go to work and let it ring when time is up. Then you are done, and if you want to do more later, you can.

I think it is really good to look at what you are and what you are not so that you can uncover. A lot of what we are talking about with this topic is who we are emerging as and who we are becoming. That is a whole different construct and a whole different concept than what we were taught to believe when we were little. My dad died right after I turned 10, and his brother, the school principal, informed me that I would go to college and get a degree in elementary education, and he would set me up for life as an elementary ed teacher in his school district, and I would never have to worry about anything. And I remember saying, 'Thanks, Uncle Dan, but I want to be a social worker.' But he was like, 'Yeah, but social workers don't make any money.' And I was like, 'That's okay. I got my calling. I know what I want to do. I want to help work with systems, and I want people to maneuver through them, and that is where I am going.' He had all the other reasons for me not to do that. But I went on, and I pursued my dreams even though I was told that I would be the first woman in the whole family not to be a teacher.

I remember sitting in my first social work class, and the professor said, 'Learn their names. That is the most important thing a person has, their name.' If you remember their name, they won't mind telling you other details because they know that they were understood. When we do business with people, the most important thing that we can do is connect with them, learn their name, look them in the eye, engage with them in social media. Don't just put a like; put a comment on what they have to say, share something that was meaningful. As Shelley can tell you, it is all about the connection, and people are buying what you offer. They are buying you. It is not just the product that sells itself, it is how the relationship is with the person that is related to that product. In my business, people can look up coaches and they all don't have the same sort of certifications that I do. They don't have the same techniques that I do. They don't have the same specialties that I do, but when somebody wants ME to be their coach, that means they want ME. Not just where I got my training, so there is something in there about who we bring to the table. I want to live in a world where I can bring all of it. I am a Jewish lesbian mother with an African-American child. I practice Zen Buddhism. I sometimes go to the Unitarian churches, and sometimes I get into the Goddess stuff and a little Wicca. I am the diversity queen over here. Diversity and inclusion. I want to bring all of my self and all of my skills to the table.

As a small business owner like I am, I'll tell you that it requires more than eight hours a day. I have the stuff I do to develop my business and the stuff I do for my clients. There is doing, and there are deliverables. But what I am always doing is practicing mindfulness. I am asking myself the question, 'Who do I want to be while I am doing what I do?' For me, mindfulness in what I am doing is making an intention for every interaction, every meeting, every whatever so that I bring my fullness and thoughtfulness to it.

A tip for all of you is three conscious breaths. Breathing is an involuntary act: As long as we breathe, we are alive. I believe that it is important to sometimes pay attention to our breath - that we are not just breathing from chin to head, but we are taking it from our bellies and sending that deep breath out. By doing three conscious breaths, especially before intense times, it helps us be more centered, more conscious and more alive to what we are doing."

J-Coby Wayne | Agent of Evolution

"I want to address productivity a bit since it's part of this topic. When we are present, productivity follows. We have talked a lot over the course of these Funday School Hangouts about the pitfalls of over-focusing on money or profit, but money is good. Money helps us do things, money is love in concretized form. When we love who we are and when we love what we are being, money is attracted to us. Whether it is through a concrete normal corporate job or whether it is in an entrepreneurial existence or whether it is in a pastoral existence, we magnetize when we are flowing who we are being, who we are meant to be. Then the productivity and the money and the brilliant ideas for planning for projects, for making them concrete and efficient, flow very effortlessly.

I want to finish up by sharing a few quotes. Annie Dillard, who wrote the book *The Writing Life*, wrote, 'The life of sensation is the life of greed; it requires more and more. The life of the spirit requires less and less.' I thought that was really brilliant for this topic. Spirit doesn't have to be spiritual. There are a lot of atheists, agnostics, non-religious, pantheistic people for whom spirit is the essence of just being. That is one of the ways that we can describe spirit in a more neutral way for those needing it to be neutral.

And here's another quote, this one from Maria Popova, creator of Brain Pickings, an online curated web service dedicated to culture. On the seventh anniversary of Brain Pickings, she wrote, 'Presence is far more intricate and rewarding an art than productivity. Productivity is a culture that measures our worth as human beings by our efficiency, our earnings and our ability to perform better in this or that. The culture of productivity has its place, but worshipping at its altar daily robs us of the very capacity of joy and wonder that makes life worth living.' And, finally, I'll finish up with Annie Dillard again. She memorably said, 'How we spend our days is, of course, how we spend our lives.'"

Shelley: "Thank you, panelists, for bringing your positive presence to our conversation today!"

Shelley's Wrap-Up

When it comes to being in a presence (being) space compared to an excessive productivity (doing) space, it's always amazing to me how everything just works as it should, when it should. We can become obsessed with timing and worrying about when and where and how, yet it seems that when you trust that things will evolve as they should, they just do... almost like magic - the alchemy of magic! Even knowing this, I cannot tell you how much time I have wasted on worrying about having enough time to finish my presentations or the Funday Hangouts that provided the content for this book. Always worrying about hurrying up so it can ALL get done and presented.

This has been a very hard habit for me to let go of. I am not sure what the lesson in this is, other than to have faith that all evolves and grows as it will. In one of my other books, I wrote about nature and how everything in nature flows in its own natural time and state - from birth to regeneration. Yet in business and in life, so many people are so very stressed (of our own doing, I might add) and waste time worrying about timing. With the Funday School Hangouts, it was amazing that with six or seven people on each panel - each having their time to talk, each being able to add something valuable during our hour together - it ALWAYS worked out to be just the perfect amount of contribution, and we always finished right on time. Call it divine intervention, or what?

Now if I can only remember this when I am presenting a Facebook class and just flow with it!

As we work on honoring being present and resonating with many of the lessons and stories shared in this hangout, we now move into principle 8 - "bring your purpose and principles into plans and projects" - to focus on ways of bringing our ideas and inspirations into practice for our business, social media and lives.

CHAPTER EIGHT

Principle #8:

Bringing Your Purpose and Principles into Plans and Projects

A couple of other ways to say this are "bringing your values into plans and projects," "bringing your philosophies into plans and projects" or "bringing your operating principles into plans and projects." (Hmmm, I like that better than "best practices"...!)

Back in Chapters 5 and 6, we talked about purpose and principles. These are great. You need them to create and sustain a conscious business. However, purpose and principles without plans and projects are pie in the sky. They don't really serve anyone if they are never translated into something tangible that is contributed out into the world and shared with others. By "tangible," I don't mean it has to be something you can see like a product or something you can "sell" like a service. I mean something real that the world and others benefit and grow from - and that you also grow from because you are fulfilling your purpose in bringing it to life.

I once worked with a company where the leaders were great at creating ideas - ideas that could change the world kinda stuff. However, they could never take these brain musings and translate them into something meaningful that could be implemented. It was a very frustrating experience because I respected the brilliance and the creation of these ideas, but without implementation, they were rainbows in the sky. Beautiful to look at and admire, but you couldn't wrap your arms around them.

This Hangout topic again brought up who I used to be when I started off my career as a teacher, counselor and school principal. I had no clue what my purpose and principles were back in my 20s. I was just in the questioning stages, and it wasn't until I was in my early 40s that I truly began to realize my purpose and awaken to the possibility of venturing out on my own. Being fired from a *Fortune* 500 company helped me get on this new path and be wide open to the possibilities ahead. Every lesson learned along life's trail brought me to where I am today. Many days, hours, weeks and years of working with great educational programs, coaches and guides helped me uncover (almost said "discover," but I think it's more of a trial-and-error and uncovering process we go through than a discovery) what I didn't want to do. And through this uncovering, you will know what feels right for you and your life. Just listen and trust in your intuition, your gut. Know that they are the barometer for your "true north." It's about being aware of energy and in harmony with the environment to create openings for energy to flow as it should and move you along the waves of living your best life.

I am now very much aware of when I am not in my "right mind," when I make decisions based on wrong anticipated outcomes. All I have to do is "choose again" when I am not living through my core values in life and best operating principles. I now operate from being aware and choosing again.

As an example of putting this into practice, let's look at when I had to create lesson plans for my fifth-grade class. I had to create a lesson plan every day for what I would be teaching, and it had to be followed to the letter. If anything went haywire - and let's face it stuff always goes awry! - it would always throw me for a loop because I didn't know how to pause, reflect, be present and choose again. Instead I would panic, be fearful and come from a place of, "Oh, my gosh, the world has ended and what am I going to do?"

Now when I am in front of a group speaking on social media and something goes haywire - which it inevitably does, especially when you are using technology - I just kind of take a breath and look at it as a gift. Whatever happens, I just try to stay present and deal with whatever it is that I am supposed to be present to.

Here's another example of staying present and flexible in the midst of plans: A week before I was writing this chapter, I had four appointments. Every single one of them had a change in time. Either they forgot about the appointment or they didn't call me. The old Shelley back in the day would have been indignant. But the conscious current Shelley was totally present to change and to how I saw the shifts in appointments. I realized, "Wow! I am so excited! I can now spend my day in nature and look at this as a gift and not be set back by what life throws at me."

What I learned from this was that the more I know my plan and my course of action (and don't get me wrong... you still have to plan; I am always well-prepared when I walk in to do a presentation or work with a client), the more the plan becomes me instead of me being the plan and being heavily invested in the plan and the outcome. It is a very different way of coming at it, and I hope this makes sense. I basically get out of the way and let my purpose and a higher energy guide me and my being during the presentation or interaction with clients and colleagues. I don't let "Shelley" get in the way - the Shelley with the ego and the baggage and the sales shark scars! I know my content and my purpose, and then I become the vehicle to deliver said material and content. But there is a higher and bigger purpose that guides me and lets me know each time I deliver a presentation that, YES, this is my gift, my purpose, my reason for being in this moment in time.

Here is an exercise that will help you bring your principles into a plan or project. Operating from your principles, set your goals and objectives. A goal is a broad-brush statement that will support the purpose and principles. An objective is a specific measurable action that supports the purpose and principles of the project or plan.

Now that you have your goal and objectives, always operating from your principles, identify how you will incorporate these into your plans and projects. Your tools or methods for setting your goals and objectives driven by your purpose and principles can vary and should fit what feels flowing and right for you.

Let me share a practical example of how I've applied what I'm recommending above. I have a Video Course to create for a public class I am delivering. So, the project is the creating of the coursework and the delivering of the created content. When I begin, I define my goal as having class attendees learn how to develop their very own video content for social media marketing. One objective would be to have 50 people registered for the class within 24 hours of start. Another objective would be to have 50% of the class create their first video and share it within 30 days of the class. In creating and delivering this class, my basic truths (principles) are always reflected. All of the principles in this book are my operating principles, and my purpose is to make a difference in life through education and always being my authentic self.

Let's see what our panelists had to say about the topic of translating "purpose and principles into plans and projects".

**Our Funday Panelists Share on
From Productivity to Presence**

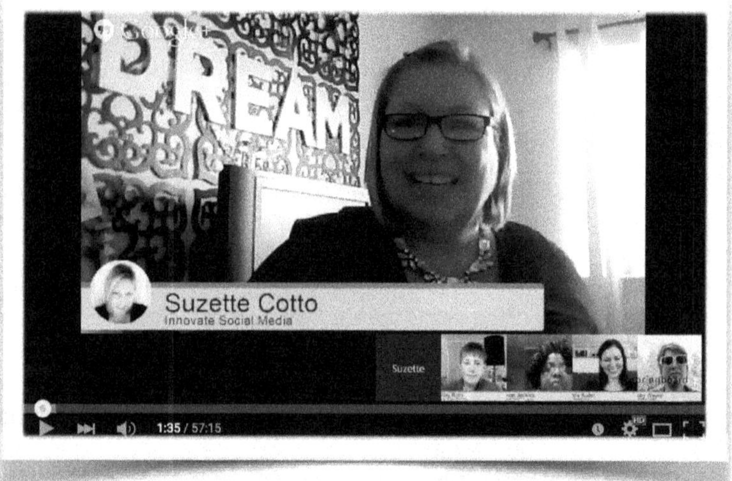

Our From Productivity to Presence Panelists

Suzette Cotto | Innovate Social Media

"I love the conversations that we have been having on the Hangouts over the past few months. They all kind of revolve around the same concepts of giving to grow and abundant exchange. This is exactly how I operate. Social media is my first real business where I have a thriving clientele and am able to continue growing. I see a lot of myself reflected in my company, and it is because of social media that I am fortunate enough to have a platform or many platforms where I get to have a voice.

One of the ways I bring my purpose and principles into plans and projects is by incorporating into my business website, a place for passion projects. Passion projects to me are things that I feel strongly about that I want to support. When you go to my website, you will see this little hand-heart diagram that takes you to a documentary I am currently working on called 'Pioneers in Skirts.' It is about providing solutions to barriers that women experience when they are getting ahead in their career. I have strong feelings about the journey of women in business and how they have grown and what they can do to continue growing. This passion is incorporated into the philosophy of who I am and the code of what makes me, me.

So I think it is important to really realize that you do have a voice. I think sometimes people go through life not realizing that they can have things that they can be passionate about and that they can incorporate them into their work life to make it much more meaningful. I wake up every day and say I am the luckiest person in the world because I get to do something that I love. This is not a cliché. Find your passion, and then pursue it and make it your job. This is how things evolved for me, and this is my take on incorporating passion and philosophy into my work life."

Sharon Jenkins | Author, Editor, Ghostwriter

"Purpose and principles are the very essence of why I do what I do. I have this keen focus on helping people deliver their written purpose. I sincerely believe that people are programmed to bring a certain message to life. Some people do it through speaking, some people do it through writing. If you do it through writing, that is where I come into play. It is my passion to educate people on what it really takes to get their books born.

Over the years, there was an evolution in my life, which meant that I would have to purify my purpose, especially in my business because my purpose is the thing that drives my business. So I had to de-clutter my self. I had to say to myself, 'Is this still valuable? Does this put fuel in my tank? Does this energize me to move forward?' I am a 'soul-opreneur,' so purpose is very important to me. It is the fuel that keeps you off of 'e' or empty when you are driving down the road of life. You have got to have something that energizes you. Before, Suzette talked about passion. To me, passion is that fuel. For me, passion is what causes you to move beyond the obstacles, the road blocks, the holes in the road. It is what gets you up and what resurrects you when you didn't fulfill that particular personal goal or that business goal.

You have to know beyond a shadow of a doubt where you are going and why you are doing something. Once you are in tune with where you are, what your purpose is and what your passion is, that is the motivation or the fuel that will keep you moving in the direction that you want to move in or that you are pre-destined to move in to."

Laine Driscoll in the audience asked:

"What are some of the awesome projects that some of you are working on right now?"

(It was agreed by Shelley and the panel that the panelists would add that into their commentaries.)

Ronda Suder | Filmmaker, Writer, Actress, Entrepreneur

When I think about this topic of bringing your principles and values to support the projects, it is important to get clear on what the principles and values are. I think we struggle sometimes with projects until we get consciously clear on what is important to us, our values, our principles. Once we get clear on these, we often look back in hindsight and say, 'Oh, that's why that project didn't work very well' or 'That's why that relationship was very difficult because it was so out of alignment with what my values and my principles are.' For me, these values and principles are bringing right relations, creativity, fun, laughter.

Because I know my values and principles, I know when something doesn't feel right, and I can always go back to those values and go back to those principles and evaluate what is out of alignment, what is not working. That may show up for me as pain in my body or lack of interest or fatigue.

Another thing that is important for me is for people to realize that it is okay for your values and principles to be different than someone else's. It's also important to get clear that your values and your operating principles are yours, and they don't have to be somebody else's. They don't have to be what someone else thinks they should be, or what you believe society thinks they should be. In work life, you may have a great job, but it has all these elements that are everyone else's values and their principles that don't work for you.

So to answer Laine's question, one of the projects I am working on is a video for an organization called Know Autism. They are very focused on bringing awareness about autism and helping support families dealing with autism.

Another project is with my work at a credit union, Primeway. The acronym at Primeway for how they conduct business is CARING. The CEO created that acronym, and she was very clear when she came in as CEO that the people - the members of the credit union - came first. Their mission is being a place where people love to work and love to do business. The company has always been about the members, and it has always been about the employees. She has never wavered on her values and what is really important to her. She didn't focus on getting short-term results. She didn't focus on short-term gratification. When she came in four years ago, she could have cut services for members to get those numbers to shift quickly, but she waited, and she really believed that if she stuck to her values and her principles and what she thought was really important, they would get the results. Four years later, they are ranked number eight in the nation on loan-to-growth and the highest on loan-to-growth ratio. This is a great example of sustainable results through plans and projects driven by purpose and principles."

Shelley commented:

"The main project I'm working on right now is taking all of our Funday School Hangouts and putting them into a book on 9 conscious principles for social media, business and life. Other projects include a big social media symposium on October 24 (2014) with five other speakers. www.shelleyroth.com is the best way to find my calendar and learn more about the projects I'm working on."

Suzette Cotto commented:

"I already mentioned the documentary film I'm involved in, 'Pioneers in Skirts.' The main thing we're focused on is trying to find company sponsors. It's a great project, but they are running on fumes right now."

Sharon Jenkins commented:

"I am currently working on a screenplay for one of my clients, who is in the financial industry, based on the television program called 'Scandal.' It has some of the same nuances, and it has turned out to be a fun project. I have also partnered with Rochelle Carter, another 'authorpreneurship' expert, to do a magazine in 2015 and to write a couple of books on authorpreneurship. Finally, I am looking at incorporating translation services into my Master Communicator business because Houston is one of the most diverse cities in the country."

J-Coby Wayne | Agent of Evolution

"I think this is one of the most important topics that we have addressed in the entire time that we have been getting together for Fundays. Purpose and principles are incredibly important, and for those of you who have been on the panel and in the audience for many of the Fundays, you know that I have participated in every single Funday from a different location around the world. That is in no small measure due to what my partner and I set out to create with our projects.

It was very clear to us when we tuned into the idea of our collaboration together through projects that adventure and playfulness and, most importantly, the vibe of 'structured flow' had to be built into every project and into our way of expressing our purpose. That strong orientation and that strong focus on what we call structured flow has really enabled us to think in a certain way, to structure things in a way that allows me to participate in Fundays from Saint John in the U.S. Virgin Islands, Maui, Los Angeles, Bodega Bay, Chicago, Rhode Island and Galveston, Texas.

I always knew when I was younger that travel, being in different locations and circulating out into the world were going to be important to me, but it wasn't until the creation of collaborative world of energy projects with my partner that we brought these to the foreground as our operating principles and purposes of our work. When we started thinking in ways to make being able to be in many different locations happen through different projects and plans, the environment and the universe around us, the ecosystem around us, responded to our clarity and pulled into our orbit the ways to make it happen. So one of the important take-aways from me for today is this concept of structured flow.

In terms of purpose and principles, I know people who are not really plagued by the question, 'What is my purpose?,' at least not consciously. For those of us who are, I didn't get the answer until I was fully ready and experienced enough to hear it, which was when I was 33 years old. For those of us who have a sense of purpose, we work really hard to figure out what it is and to identify our craft. But we can't stop there. For some people, having a dream internally is enough to fuel us. But a lot of us who are creative want to share that dream out and turn it into something that is experienced by others. My partner's name for this topic today is 'from impression to expression,' which is brilliant. The purpose part is the impression. We get impressed, we plug into this impression, this strong energy and idea. This is the purpose. The purpose translates into principles, which we connect with by being impressed by the things that we see around us regarding what's valued, what are considered truths, what we won't participate in like what Ronda was talking about and realizing that our principles are often different from what other people consider either normal or acceptable or valuable.

We have all this stuff impressed on us, but then where we have a real responsibility is translating our purpose and principles into something that resonates, into something that has impact. This is the expression part. I am not putting a definition on impact here because there is no universal definition of impact. For me, if I draw a picture and I like the result or in some way resonate with the results, that may be all the impact that I want or need to have. I am not out to be a visual artist as a career, but for other people who do their art with an absolute need for an audience, their definition of impact through their art will be different from mine based on the purpose of doing the art.

It is really part of our responsibility and part of our purpose as human beings to be stewards of creative energy and the creative faculty. Structured flow has been a very important way for me to bring the capacity of impression (the creativity faculty) to expression into life through plans and projects because sometimes our dreams start to lose their luster and a little of their juice when we have to plan. We may start to feel like, 'This sucks! I am going to have to put walls around my dream to give it structure.' This is probably what Suzette's Pioneers in Skirts project is dealing with. You can have a marvelous, important concept and project, but when you start running on fumes, it is really difficult to keep finding the original juice of the inspiration, especially if people aren't sharing or buying into the vision of the universal principle that you would think is a no-brainer.

So I have found in my work that structured flow is a really good way of turning impression into expression because it gives you some sort of form, but it is a loose, organic structure that also enables flow. That is the balancing point that we all need to find between flow and letting inspiration bonk us on the head. Sometimes we hit dry patches, and the reason isn't because we are not on the right path or we are not doing our right purpose. It is often because we are in a part of our path and our manifesting where we are having to call on ourselves and our creative resources to develop more creativity and resourcefulness within ourselves.

Let me turn now to Laine's question of the awesome projects that I am working on. A main project I'm focused on right now is the quarterly online Weeks of World Cooperation. These online Weeks of World Cooperation that I am part of hosting make up one of the tangible projects and ways that I bring the world of energy (one of my greatest purposes) to life. I am part of this massive purpose and principle of sharing that everything is energy and evolves through energy together, but how do we turn that huge thing into a project and a plan?

The way that we have turned it into a project and a plan is by offering a way to think about navigating this world by bringing world cooperation to life through one week four times a year via the Internet. For the Week of World Cooperation that I happen to be in the middle of hosting right now, the purpose is to bring the reality that everything is energy to life. The principle is that we all, as human beings, are agents of evolution. We start the first day of the Cooperation Week event with this principle. Then the rest of the days of the week go through concrete ways (plans/

projects) of being agents of evolution, from world citizenship to world meditation to world cooperation to world service to world impression to world wisdom to world regeneration.

This is a structure (plan/project) that we have been using and testing out for three years personally and through how we do our collaborative work. In the fourth year, we have arrived at being able to create a well-crafted package, project and plan for the general public. We have used structured flow to do this, so for me this has been a great experience and concrete example of a process to bring the power to manifest to life by turning purpose and principles into plans and projects. And this power is human beings' unique special ability, gift, service and role in the world as stewards of the creative faculty."

Shelley: "Thanks for the lively discussion, panelists!"

Shelley's Wrap-Up

These Funday School Hangouts really revealed and reinforced that the projects all the "Fundayers" work on bring our purpose and principles into being. It's at the heart of why we do the things we do, and it brings us a lot of meaning through concrete and practical ways of making a difference in the form of plans and projects. After getting aware of identifying, bringing purpose to and delivering on our projects, we focused our last Funday School session on how we define and measure the assets in our businesses and lives.

C H A P T E R   N I N E

Principle #9:

Reinventing Company Assets

In the "From Profits to Principles" chapter (Chapter 6), we asked our panelists what success looks like in their business. In our last Hangout together, we asked them:

How do you measure value and "success" in your business and life?

It was very fitting that this hangout happened close to Halloween, and a few of us came in costume to celebrate. Fun and the ability to express ourselves freely and without inhibition or fear of being judged or laughed at proved to be two of the most important and valuable assets I, the panelists and the audience shared, enjoyed and benefitted from during our time together in these Funday hangouts.

In today's world, a company's assets or a worker's value are not all about the bottom line. As I've shared throughout this book, for too long, I thought they were, and I was driven to be one of the best sales sharks on the planet. I definitely fulfilled that objective. I saw the world on the company's dime.

Now, however, there is a different perspective, a different way, a different feeling and energy. Why do a majority of companies still measure success by the traditional bottom line of profits? Why don't we have other measurements on the annual report showing new ways of evaluating a business's success or lack thereof? Companies love metrics. The traditional attitude has been, "If we can't measure it, how do we know how we are doing?" That's a reasonable question. And so corporations, companies, the stock market and government regulators keep using the metric of sales/profits/growth/ income as the main measuring stick for success in business.

But what if we could measure success in other ways? What if we could show other assets on our company and personal bottom line that might not be measured in the traditional sense? How about health? With healthcare costs skyrocketing, you would think businesses would be most concerned with a healthy workforce and showing the savings on medical expenses via healthy employees as a true asset. The asset becomes "fit" employees who don't need traditional medical care for traditional medical ailments.

In a perfect world, money as a currency will continue to morph into social and relationship currency... It's not all about the deal; it's about caring about your community, your city, your planet. This has become my businesses culture that I stand for... and what my book and future will embrace. This was our last Funday session, and our first! This is not the end, but the beginning of bringing this work to other business owners and employees, starting in Houston and working outward. So stay tuned.

"Business as usual" doesn't need to be the way anymore. Business as Unusual will be the norm!

What is the meaning of success?

I challenge you to rethink your answers to that question and create a list of measureable assets in your business, projects or life that go beyond traditional profitability.

List your assets in an annual report even if the structure of your endeavor or projects doesn't require you legally to have one. To do this, you have to ask:

- **What are my Company or Project (and Life) Assets?**
- **How do I measure and define my Company or Project (and Life) Assets?**
- **What do I (and my company) truly value, and how will I measure it?**

So many peeps have good ideas, but how do you bring ideas into expression? Businesses give us a means to bring these ideas into expression, but money is not the only means of currency, especially as more of society is moving towards living for meaning and not just for money, living for real relationships and lasting connection and not just for a quick buck, living for a healthy future for all and not just a "use-it-all-for-me now" that considers no future quality for anyone. A next very real corporate and personal asset or currency is the substance and degree of consciousness in anything being created or done. Consciousness of money, consciousness of time, consciousness of the quality of attention, consciousness of the long-term impact for communities and generations to come.

Here are 10 company, project and life assets I consider important. I hope they'll be a springboard for your own creative thinking about what's important to you, how you will bring the assets that are important to you into your culture and how you measure progress going forward. As we do this, let's remember that the new ROI is Return on Influence, and sometimes the influence we have can't be measured by traditional means.

1. ***Profits for shareholders, for employees, for employees' families and for suppliers or partners***

Some of the most common already-existing forms of this are: **co-ops** where a group of individuals - often the founders, managers, employees and customers - are owners and stakeholders with mutual interest in the company and **ESOPS** (which stands for "employee stock ownership plan").

Some co-ops you might have heard of include ACE Hardware, Associated Press (media), Blue Diamond Growers (nut growers), Land 'O Lakes (butter), Ocean Spray (juice and fruit), REI (outdoor gear and adventure), Sunkist Growers Inc. (juice and fruit), True Value Corporation (hardware) and Wheatsville Co-op (natural grocer), an Austin, Texas institution.

Some ESOPs you might know of include Avis Rent-a-Car, Bob's Red Mill (natural, organic, gluten-free grain products such as flours), CH2M Hill (engineering), Ferrellgas Partners (natural gas), Herman Miller (office furniture), King Arthur Flour (one of the conscious businesses we interviewed for Chapter 10), Publix Super Markets and W.W. Norton & Company (publishers).

If you own a company or work for a company and are interested in exploring extending profits to employees, you can research co-ops and ESOPs just by doing a search online. We've provided some links in the Resources appendix.

2. ***Time donated to causes and/or charities and/or to people in need***

PRACTICE:

Carve out time. From solopreneurs to big companies, it's setting aside time for employees or individuals on a recurring basis to give of themselves during company hours. Additionally, having employees contribute financially through payroll deductions, if they opt to do that, is also a fairly effortless way to donate to causes or charities or people.

3. ***Employees' time spent in nature communing and getting to know how they integrate with all aspects of life***

   It's been shown that some of the most creative innovations and solutions come from connecting disparate dots, especially through interacting with the natural world outside an office or work. Albert Einstein was said to have noodled extensively on his Theory of Relativity while sailing.

   PRACTICE:

   Field trips. We did it in elementary school. Why don't companies have field trips? That would be a really cool way to help people appreciate - because you're paying them to appreciate - the inspirations of nature. You never know what can open up from there.

   I have a memory that one of the things I did as a teacher was that I took the kids outside and no one could talk. We could only listen to the sounds of nature so that we could hear what we never hear because we're so busy inside. That experience was an eye-opener even for me to be quiet and just listen - whether it was nature sounds or man-made sounds. It really gives you room for pause on the interconnectedness of everything.

   We are so entrapped in being busy and busy being productive. We so discount silence and getting outside the well-greased machine of productivity that we don't leave an opening for new thoughts and feelings and ideas to occur. Just as diversity has been in the spotlight for the last ten years, it's the same with nature. Try opening up your company to other ways of being "productive" that aren't traditional - whether a field trip to a museum or to a forest or to the beach. Wouldn't it be cool to measure how many experiences you've given your employees outside the company?

When you take people outside their familiar environments, it creates opportunities for new ways to connect the dots and new ways of thinking about radically creative and even revolutionary ways for solving problems and creating solutions. From my experience, one of the most powerful team-building exercises was traveling to Europe with a group of co-workers on a sales quota club. The opportunity to be with people that we took for granted through our related-ness inside the company opened up when we were in a different realm. There was a whole new appreciation for our inter-connectedness outside in a new environment. The bonding was incredible. It forced us to be in a social situation, and not in the same "having to be productive" environment. This created a deeper level of understanding and support of each other from that shared experience, so going forward, we all became more multidimensional, and there was more respect among each other in work collaborations.

One of the ways we could measure this would be for each department to track increases/decreases in something measurable that may be affected by the added experience of field trips. An example may be in the Human Resources department. Before and after an experience, they could note how many new applications were received for open positions in the company, and track the quality of those applicants pre- and post-experience. In addition, a survey tool could be used to garner the opinions of the employees' attitudes of the company pre- and post-field activities.

4. ***Employees' time spent acknowledging other co-workers and clients, prospects, etc. outside of business as usual***

PRACTICE:

Contribute positive input. I remember that at work eveyone would talk about their family, but I had a different lifestyle, so I could never be myself inside a company because I couldn't share myself. I'm not talking about asking employees to go drinking and do some "rah-rah" stuff outside of work. There was always such competition among people, we never got to acknowledge other people because we were coming from scarcity. I think it would be pretty amazing if, as employees and partners, we were incented to recognize a strength in someone else and have to share that on a quarterly basis. It would be especially interesting and important to acknowledge - in sales, for instance - a strength or quality or contribution outside of work of those salespeople who AREN'T hitting their targets as much. Everyone on that sales team contributes and can be recognized for their contribution, not just their contribution to the traditional bottom line.

Each sales meeting, where numbers are reported, have every person share a concrete measurable activity they may have participated in that was outside of their sales role. An example would be to honor those who have donated time, money and/or expertise to non-profits or casuses or who participated in an interest outside of work such as creating a piece of art or cycling 100 miles in one trek or hiking into a challenging and remote camping area to take beautiful photographs of sites most people never get to see. This could be measured and valued and brought into existence in every meeting, be it sales, research and development and other divisions of the company.

For clients and vendors, select a client and a vendor each month or quarter and highlight one of their strengths or contributions and feature them in your company newsletter or on your Facebook business page. Giving recognition to non-traditional contributions is a way to set the example for others to follow. Just like a pebble dropped in a pond, the ripples will resonate outward.

A happy, healthy employee =
a happy, healthy company!

5. ***Time spent by employees and team members focusing on their healthy lifestyle***

PRACTICE:

Provide onsite facilities outside of normal company job functions such as a library, gym, outside nature preserve and online classes and encourage and reward employees and team members or partners for actually using these facilities and options. As I've shared, at the software company where I worked, all those things were there, but no one used them because people were afraid of being viewed as not productive. The company culture didn't encourage that behavior. Part of getting people to let go of fear of being judged as "non-productive" is by making it mandatory in an employee's day or week to take something like three hours a week and giving them company-provided or company-suggested options for what do with their time. You don't have to be a large company to implement this practice. The optional activities could be outside the company walls. Here might be some choices: go to the gym, go to the library, go to a local nature preserve, take a class, join a choir. Anything that may contribute to both physical health and mental health.

Have the employee or team member track activities with a daily spreadsheet or journal. Each time they do one of these activities, they note what their main experience was and how they then applied that experience or inspiration in their work. That journal is shared with their supervisor or manager (or with yourself or an accountability buddy if you're the boss) once a quarter or at the end of the year. The leader of a company - even a solopreneur - shares their "inspiration journal" via social media and/or at the annual meeting or quarterly meetings as part of how they've contributed to the progress and culture and work of the company for that year.

MEASUREMENT:

This measurement would be over a period of time and would be a moving average. Medical expenses for employees and team members would have to be tracked and compared over time. A line chart showing costs, both time and money, for each employee and/or department would be created and tracked. Comparisons would be made to pre- and post-program implementation, and then the savings in time and money would be shown on the annual report.

6. ***Laughter and fun***

Me bringing laughter and fun in my Orange Is The New Black Halloween Costume during our Hangout on Halloween day

PRACTICE:

Lighten up the workday. One of the practices when I was in education was that the principal would get on the Public Address system and share the customary announcements. Why not liven up the company and do a mid-day announcement via email or text sharing a joke or a funny video or something positive trending in the news? Work is hard, and bringing levity to the work day via laughter is important. This would be a mandatory practice and could be delegated to various individuals in each department that want to contribute. It could be daily or weekly or monthly, depending on the size of the company and the number of volunteers to organize and contribute a mid-day moment of levity and laughter.

Another practice can be to feature employees' and team members' pets as the "VP of Morale" for the month. The featured pet would be picked randomly and circulated via newsletter and social media. This encourages fun and participation, and we all love our pets!

MEASUREMENT:

For this practice and all of the others, the financial bottom line, customer satisfaction survey tools, lower health care costs and other measures inside departments could be tracked. This practice would have a positive effect on the many of the traditional measurements inside of a company, in addition to improved customer service reviews, more engagement on social media and increased growth of the contact database. Who wouldn't want to be on the email list that is sharing the monthly pet VP of Morale?! So much fun!

7. Time spent in balance with family and friends

I think more companies give flex-time, but there isn't always a culture that supports it. So many people bank their flex-time and never use it, for fear of being judged. Make it so that employees can't carry flex-time over to encourage them to spend time with family and friends. Companies could actively pay their employees to go watch their kids' performances and Little League games and participate at their children's schools. Ideas for encouraging this behavior would be to provide time during the business week to go be with their kids in school; have an option to bring your pet to work; have a dog park on the premises; have employees invite family members to dine with them at lunch and break time; schedule creative time to be with family, friends or co-workers; invite family members of employees to mentor other employees or contribute to focus groups and brainstorm new ideas for new services or products or problems the company is working on. Why pay big consulting companies for this when you may have wealth of information inside your employees and their families? Finally, consider onsite day care centers where the grandparents are brought in to help be with the kids.

8. ***Accountability***
9. ***Trust***
10. ***Authenticity***

MEASUREMENT:

Accountability, trust and authenticity are all related and can be measured via a customer service survey tool used quarterly that includes questions that reflect how the company is doing in those areas. When authoring my first book, *Get Real, People!*, we developed a measurement app to get at evaluating a personal or business social media post's accountability, trustworthiness and authenticity. It was going to produce a measure of how "real" a person was being in their social media communication via their status updates, blog posts,"about section company descriptions," blogs, brochures and more.

The vision for the app was to determine how authentic a person or business was via measurement of words being used that set off the "Real-O-Meter." The app could be a method for getting at accountability, trust and authenticity via the printed word. I realized that digital body language (i.e., what we make up about people and companies via their online "look" and communication) is huge! We interviewed many people to determine what we "make up" when we do not see a picture on a personal profile on LinkedIn, for example, or when someone doesn't post anything for six months on their Facebook business page.

This was a real eye-opener. In our research, we found levels of trust were diminished and negative feedback ensued when not doing social media the "right way." Old habits for old sales sharks and even just good old business dogs seem hard to break based on years of business as usual.

With the right developer, the Real-O-Meter may in fact be a measurement tool that will be used to measure a company's trust level and authenticity via digital body language online. Online words, communication, "tone of voice" all affect digital body language and how you and your business are perceived.

In creating the Real-O-Meter, we generated a list of words and phrases that were a set of potential positives and potential negatives. Then we weighted them, also subjectively, from 0-100 on a scale of "realness" where low-scoring words were interpreted as less real, and high-scoring words were interpreted as super-real.

Once developed, the app will search out the social media entries you select to apply it to such as blogs or Facebook profile or status updates, and it will note the frequency of any of the words or phrases in the Real-O-Meter index. After doing some calculations, it will return back an assessment on the Real-O-Meter dial graphic, noting whether that entry rates as authentic or not. The original goal of the app was to help make us aware of what is truly heart-centered versus self-promotional in our digital media communications.

The app is not complete because we're still looking for the right developer, so anyone with technical software development and program-ming skills that resonates with the Real-O-Meter app and would like to work with us, please do email me at sroth@shelleyroth.com.

Here's some other information from my *Get Real, People!* book about being authentic and qualitative ways to measure it.

THE REAL FACTOR

How do you know if you are being real?
What does it mean to be real?

"Real" according to dictionary.com and Wikipedia is:

genuine; not counterfeit, artificial, or imitation; authentic; unfeigned or sincere

Synonyms include:

natural, true, genuine, not artificial, not fake, heartfelt, authentic, actual

Antonyms (opposites) include:

imaginary, unreal, fictitious, make-up,
pretend, feigned, sham, staged,
artificial, counterfeit, fake

To know if you (or someone else) is being real or authentic (and, by extension, trustworthy and accountable), the first check I would suggest is to check your physical reaction to what you are doing. Do you have an enhanced or sensitive sense of self (i.e., heart rate, tightness, feeling "off")? These can be indicators that something is not right. Your physical body is a bellwether for knowing if you are being real. Most of us don't "listen" to our physical indicators as we are buried in "noise" pollution all around us. We also discount these indicators thinking that we must play a certain role, be a certain way, so "suck it up" and just don't listen to our higher selves, which tend to inform our physical bodies. We just have to trust to listen to them.

I know if I am being real when it is effortless. When I am in the flow. When "Shelley" steps out of the way and a higher source is flowing through me and just being.

Online, it really becomes a challenge to be real and listen to your bodily reactions to others. We all have this higher self, this higher filter. It's just a matter of tuning into it. When you are communicating online, are you "in the flow?" Are you sensitive to how your words might land on someone? Are you thinking about "am I trying too hard to sell something/someone?"

For me, many of my colleagues in the past told me that their perception of me was that I was curt, short, not caring. This is really nothing new. I was told this by friends, family and co-workers most of my adult life. Even though I am a nurturer, I am also a businessperson, and many people throughout my career and sometimes even today have construed my directness and my business-like manner for not caring. This couldn't be further from the truth. I do have to be aware of this, especially on social media, because if the goal is to be who you are without excluding anyone, then being aware of how you are being perceived is very important, including online.

We've covered the physical body and its reaction to "not real." Now, it's also a good idea to listen to your emotional sense and see what surfaces. There is nothing that makes my emotions go off the chart like seeing a status update, email or anything that is so twentieth-century by using all the "business-as-usual" keywords like "buy now," last chance," "one day only!," "act now"... and on and on. This is very old-school marketing and just doesn't work online because it's not REAL! So listen to how your emotions react when reading about people and their business, and trust your emotional self to tell you when something just doesn't ring true.

Usually your first reaction is the REAL YOU. Trust in the REAL FACTOR!

Let's stop striving for the metric of more and focus on the metric of meaning!

Before I wrap up my piece of this chapter, let's see what the panelists had to say about "reinventing company assets." I asked them to share what they find valuable in their businesses and how they measure that.

Our Funday Panelists Share on Reinventing Company Assets

Our Reinventing Company Assets Panelists

Sharon Jenkins | Author, Editor, Ghostwriter

"In thinking about reinventing company assets, I think about the question, 'What does success look like in my business?' I believe the word 'impact' is the way to define how I measure success in my business. Am I having an impact in my industry? Am I having an impact in the lives of my clients and customers? Am I having an impact in the world? Am I having an impact in my life? What kind of impact is my writing service bringing to me? I believe that what you sow into the earth is what comes back to you. So am I sowing good seeds in my industry and into the lives of my customers? At the end of the year, I measure my impact according to my longstanding relationships and what my customers say about the service that I rendered to them. What kind of impact did my service have on their lives, on their businesses? What does my service render them in the marketplace in their industry? That is how I measure what I do with regard to business."

Shari Joyce | Divine Consultant and Founder & Chief Spiritual Officer

"Thinking about this topic on what I value and how I measure it, I decided to focus on Corporate Social Responsibility (CSR). Corporate social responsibility is a way for our business or social organizations to show that they care for our local communities and the environment as a way of giving back. One way that is obvious is to donate profits to various causes. I choose to be a bit more hands-on by doing things like joining committees for community projects. Volunteering my time is the asset that I have more to give right now than money. Whatever it is you have to give - your time, talent, treasure - I would encourage you to donate it.

Another thing that I do is pass along our old technology equipment. So if you have an old office computer or a laptop lying around, you can donate it to a local school to assist students in learning. This also goes for old office supplies and furniture. The way I do this through my company is that I am the board secretary for the Surplus Exchange, which is a non-profit where we prevent waste from entering landfills by taking surplus out from businesses and donating it to churches and to universities. We can measure the value of this for companies that donate by giving them a report on what their diversion weight was. This is very important because they have to report their diversion weights to their jurisdictions. Let me give you an example of this type of measurement. Through this program in California, we diverted over 150 pounds from the landfill. We also have recycled over 20,000 pounds of heavy waste and over 21,000 pounds of heavy metal. So that is all a part of Corporate Social Responsibility.

Larger mortar and brick companies can do things like a bike incentive to reduce their carbon footprint by encouraging their employees to cycle to work. In your own business, you can try to use green suppliers and local suppliers, which cuts down on delivery miles and helps reduce the carbon footprint. I try to use recycled products as much as possible in my business - everything from inks to batteries to light bulbs. My business cards are printed on recycled paper. In this way, I walk my talk, and I think that is very important.

Another benefit and measurable value of thinking in terms Corporate Social Responsibility is that I have met new clients while I was volunteering at a fundraiser. You will tend to meet people of like mind when you choose to donate your time to a cause you care about. Another thing I do is to donate a portion of what clients choose to pay me to a charity or a non-profit. I ask them if there is one that they work with, that they would like to donate the money to, and that gets them involved in the process in a way. So what I've shared today are some of the non-traditional corporate assets I value and how I put them into practice in measurable ways."

Shelley commented:

"These Funday School hangouts are donation- based. The donations are going to one of my passions, which is land conservation because we can't ever replace the land and nature. It is another line item to see how much a corporation is giving, not just in money, but also in 'time, talent and treasure' as Shari said."

J-Coby Wayne commented:

"When I sang with the United Nations Association International Choir in Houston, one of the things that was really cool was that members of the choir who were with corporations had matching programs. Their time in the choir was considered volunteer time by their companies. We had three-hour rehearsals once a week and longer ones once a month, and basically every hour that they racked up singing was donated as corresponding funds back to the choir by companies like Exxon and Marathon. So even though the oil companies sometimes get a bad rap outside of Houston, they generated a lot of revenue for the choir that enabled us to do things that we would not have been able to do otherwise."

Courtney Coates | Social Media Manager

"To me success is kind of simple. I love doing what I do. I do social media management for a few clients in North Houston, Texas. I am a mom of two, and last year, I was Miss Volunteer of the Year! PTO, PTA, you name it, I did it! But I pulled off that hat, and I said, 'Let me focus on my business.' I am now coming to the end of my first year in business. The way I measure myself is really kind of crazy because my goal has been to perfect my business model and work more efficiently, charge more money and spend less time working.

Success to me is sitting on the couch watching the Saints kick butt last night. I am an artist. I am a graphic designer by degree, so when I get the feeling of 'I love this' or 'This is amazing' or 'Gosh, you are so good,' that to me is personal success because I feel like I can put my heart and soul into what I do, because I am not just doing a job. It is my skill, that's my artwork in there.

I took on a client last year, a wine bar here in The Woodlands. It started very basic, just posting media to their Facebook and Twitter, but it evolved to where they really depended on me. Therefore, I was able to charge them more money, but I was able to do what they were requesting in less time, and I have seen them succeed with this model. I feel like I have succeeded on their behalf. And that gives me goose bumps. I love that. I love that they give my name out, so one good job leads to another. I have gotten to the point that I am selective in who I want to work for, and I only work for people who are going to bring me to the next level."

Shelley commented:

"It is fun to hear other people on the panel because I personally would never think about a measure of success as my free time, but what a great measure of success! That free time can be used to give you whatever brings you more energy to do what you are passionate about. That's something I would have never thought about as a line item on a corporate spread sheet."

Sharon Jenkins commented:

"I have been observing the younger generation, those in their 20s and 30s (I am proud to say that I am 57), and they all love taking it easy! They like enjoying life, and I think we can learn from them! And I think in the future, as they start stepping up to the plate and really start doing something about the business world, we will see them incorporating things into business that allow you to take a break and enjoy life. I welcome that because I have seen people die at their desks and jumping out of windows because something happened in the stock market. I have seen professionals on 12 medications due to the stress in their jobs because the competition and bullying are so fierce that you fear for your life. So I love the fact that with this younger generation, we are going towards a place where we can go, 'Ahh, sigh' in the business world. I think that is really cool."

Shelley commented:

"I believe that if you are passionate about what you do, it becomes not work and it just becomes being. When I am in front of people training them and helping them grow through Funday School principles or social media practices, it is not work. Many of these people that are in corporate America just work to the bone without having balance in their lives. The younger generation demands when they go in for an interview that it is a company that values balance so that whatever time they have, they can give back or use to be a better person and a better contributor in their life."

J-Coby Wayne | Agent of Evolution

"I have found that with any person or enterprise, the currency that we value changes over time. The concept of success isn't in my vocabulary anymore. Value is the next evolution of the concept of success, but success was the most important currency to me throughout my entire life up until a certain point. Coming from a family with high expectations and having a nature where I placed high expectations on myself, success was first defined for me in nursery school. Then it was defined as success in kinder-garten. Then it was defined in riding competitions. Then it was defined by success at getting a date in high school, which I sucked at. Then it was defined as success in getting into Brown University. Then it was defined as success in getting into Harvard University. Then I got out into the real world, and I had no idea how to define my success or what I wanted to do with my life.

I came out of undergraduate university in 1988 and then grad school in 1991. That was the 'greed is good' Wall Street era and culture, which is so contrary to my being that it was a very painful time to be a young person getting a job in the professional market. Part of the problem was that those who had a pedigree-type mind were going to Wall Street, and Ivy League graduates like me were expected to go to high-paying type jobs. That was so not me! I studied international relations, literature, languages. I traveled all over the world. I was interested in cultures. I had studied art history. For me, money wasn't what was important, and I didn't consider it a measure of having 'made it.'

Even though it was very important to me to apply my mind to making a difference and solving big global challenges, my most important currency in those days instead of money was status or recognition. I came out of all of these schools expecting to have the corner office and the best computer. I expected to have all of my good grades recognized. Up until that point in my life, things had come pretty easily, and my constant measuring stick was if I was being recognized. My currency and measurement of 'success' were completely determined by how others perceived me. But status as a currency ended up not working for me too well in the real world because I didn't fit into corporate boxes, and I wasn't valued as much in my early jobs as I expected to be. I realized that valuing status might not get me very far because I tended not to fit traditional definitions of success. This was accompanied by a sense that I didn't fit traditional definitions of beauty. I have a big Hungarian nose and big Hungarian ears. I thought I looked like a guy, and I never fit in with the perky, blonde, Farah Fawcett look that was valued throughout my youth.

Fast forward, and I was burned out at the age of 28. I had achieved every goal that I had set for myself by that age, but I was working 22-hour days. It was just horrible, so the universe and my internal guidance system caused me to blow out my knee skiing and really start redefining my currencies and what I valued. Fast forward again many years, and I realized that the currency I valued most was adventure. Now, for me, being able to spend three weeks in Chicago for the International Film Festival and two organ concerts and the David Bowie exhibit at the Museum of Contemporary Arts is way more valuable than any money anybody can pay me.

In terms of business, I believe that the future is really coming up with accounting practices, corporate policies and government policies that allow for the injecting of new creative ways to measure 'value' in addition to profit. Part of the issue now is that we don't have tax codes that measure or incent anything other than profit. Whether we like it or not, it won't be until large corporations take on new models, expanded models - not only providing gym memberships and volunteer days, but also measuring that impact on the bottom line, which some of them are starting to do - that things will really change. Things will also change from the ground up with the Millennials saying, 'We are not going to work this way.' Eventually, there won't be anyone who wants to work at a business-as-usual corporation, and that will change things as well.

Finally, one of the most highly stable structures in the universe, is a stool - a three-legged object. This points to a reality in business that will reinvent concepts of company assets when this reality is recognized. In this structure of three, we have a universal life cycle - whether it is a company or an entrepreneur or an individual. There is a phase where we are creating, creating, creating. Then after we have created, there is a phase of preserving. This is the preservation of what has been created, the feeding and watering. Then there is a destruction phase like the wildfire in the forest that allows sunlight to come in for the next phase of growth.

This presents a challenge to the way things are currently valued in terms of profit. Every project or corporation needs to go through a phase that is highly creative, then a preservation phase where a lot of money is being made, and then comes a natural and necessary clearing phase where you are clearing out the dead wood of the project or a person's life that is obsolete and no longer serves. It's similar to singing: There are times when you are singing out, and then there are interludes and rests that are more quiet. This is when you are inhaling. In business, this is a time when you may be 'losing money' in the conventional terms of the balance sheet. But more accurately in terms of reinvented company, project and life assets and thinking, you are flowing or exchanging money out.

The stock exchange and the quarterly reporting valuing only shareholder profit creates this insane expectation and pressure for things to constantly be going up and up and up and up in corporations, but that's not the way life works. It is a wrong and unnatural value. Even for us individually, there are times when we should not be working hard. There are times we should be resting. There are times when we should be contemplating and thinking, but not expressing. There are times when we should be relating to people, but not so much focusing on making money.

A lot of us follow these rhythms naturally or instinctually, but this understanding needs to be built more into classrooms.

There are times when kids should not be constantly in their heads. There are times to be in their bodies. There are times to be building their hearts. I came out of all these high-faluting universities with a big old head, but with not much of an ability to relate one-on-one because I cared more about the world and society on a large scale than I did about individual people.

This imbalance of up, up, up, up, up, which is contrary to nature, has to break eventually, and in the aftermath of that, there need to be people who are ready with the capacity to measure value in new ways, who can start creating these measures. In the meantime, we can start in our own ways by finding ways for people to see and value those alternative currencies we've discussed today like free time, volunteer time, the ability to walk in nature, the ability to adventure... I've recently experienced that I plug into brilliant ideas when I am watching people surf. Now what employer, what corporation - maybe Google or GoPro - would allow me and pay me to go out and watch surfers all day in order to create the next big thing?"

Shelley commented:

"You are so right, J-Coby. We call ourselves lazy if we are just sitting back, and I am guilty of this myself. It is like I always feel like I need to be productive. It is almost like learned behavior coming up through kinder-garten all the way up - produce, produce. But who's to say when I am sitting back in my back forty, my little piece of heaven, by the creek behind my house in the woods, communing with nature, that the energy I am putting out and giving back isn't going to make me a better social media guide? Ebb and flow is what it is all about. I really do believe that we need to come up with a new balance sheet. I never even thought about the tax perspective, and how to have a new tax structure. Somehow we have to measure how we embrace our consciousness. Maybe it is the time donated to causes. Maybe it is the employee spending more time on the beach watching surfers so they are inspired to create. Maybe it is laughter. Maybe it is fun. Maybe the new balance sheet has trust on it, authenticity, being who you are without trying to be someone else. Accountability can be a currency.

This has been our last Funday School for Business Hangout, so I would like to share that moving forward, Funday School will continue to live through my upcoming book, and I am creating workshops and seminars to bring this knowledge to other individuals and companies as I strive to bring new thinking and ways to measure success going forward in business."

Shelley: "Thank you, panelists and audience participants, for a great and valuable nine months of conversation about conscious business. This book couldn't have happened without you!"

Shelley's Wrap-Up

What's valuable to me is imparting knowledge to businesspeople that helps them grow personally and in business. What's really valuable is watching the popcorn kernels pop... Seeing people get it. Helping people see that it's not all about money, that there is so much more to value. The people you are serving are increasingly not seeing money as what's valuable. It might be how you listened to them or the time you give them or what causes you are supporting or donating to. Different people value different things. If I post an image on my Facebook page and share a picture of a beautiful deer in a park, more people may value the picture of the deer than the social media tip I posted earlier. We as humans want to be a part of, to laugh, to participate. We all value many different things, and often, the more personal - which is perceived as more real - the better.

Other currencies besides money are: humor, laughter, visual reward, spiritual energy, digital body language, nature, animals, charities, freedom, creativity. Here's a formula that I've developed in this new world transformed by social media:

70% of the time, you're building relationships.

+

20% of the time, you're sharing other people's stuff and giving to grow.

+

10% of the time, you're actually talking about your business or offering a special.

People value that you give them a piece of YOU! But how do you value that? It's about building trust. It's about engaging and building relationships. The money will follow, no doubt - or maybe not necessarily the money, but whatever you value most, you will attract. I think money is a natural by-product when you are being a conscious business and conscious businessperson bringing the 9 principles shared in this book to life.

If you have high energy and inspiration around a particular "company asset," this is an indicator that bringing that company asset to your business and your life is a good next step. It's totally your experience. Social media has brought into mass and public consciousness that social and relationship assets are more and more important to people and need to be for businesses as well. What is your social currency?

This is an area - "additional other assets" - that people need to know. Considering "time" as a company asset is a next step of currency or asset for many people and businesses. Another next-step currency after time is "quality of attention given." When you bring these new balance sheet assets to life through your business and your relationships, you are helping businesses not just value what they've been told to value. You are leading by example. Consider thinking outside the box as you embark on implementing some of our 9 principles for conscious business, social media and life. Pick one or two and start to think about and measure creatively how they are impacting you, your team members, the company, the community and the world!

Don't be afraid to speak up and speak out. Our world needs you and your thoughts and creative ideas. New ways of measurement are just around the corner, and our balance sheets in life and in business will be transformed.

Thanks for reading this book. Thanks for being open to growth. Join us on Facebook via www.shelleyroth.com, and check out our calendar of upcoming seminars on the 9 principles. Let us know how you are doing and share your outside-the-box company (or project and life) assets and measurements so we can all enjoy being the best we can be for ourselves and our world!

Here's a last thought and practice to help you reinvent company assets:

We've been considering expanding what gets included in a company's balance sheet and assets, so why not do the same for employees and team members?

PRACTICE/MEASUREMENT:

Try keeping a list of what you, as an employee, team member or company owner value in your company work day. It might be time off, financial perks, health care, gym membership or, if you are thinking way outside the box, how about having your child's college tuition paid for? Check out CEO, Chieh Huang, of Boxed and this amazing perk he gives employees - full tuition to college for their children! www.huffingtonpost.com/2015/05/26/boxed-college-tuition-ben_n_7445644.html?ncid=fcbklnkushpmg00000063.

While some companies offer to pay tuition for workers, funding workers' kids is pretty rare outside of academia. Starbucks and Chrysler recently announced programs to cover workers' college tuition bills, but those benefits are far more restrictive, and both companies will only foot the bill at hand-picked schools.

Create two balance sheets - one for your company and one for yourself! Assign some sort of scale to your personal balance sheet line items to measure how much you have "accrued" or experienced each line item that quarter or year like 1-5 with 1 being not accrued or experienced much and 5 being highly accrued or experienced. Then create a section of your annual report that reports your "personal values earnings" (PVE). Have fun creating a look and feel for your PVE balance sheet: Maybe it's super-conventional so it looks just like a regular balance sheet, or maybe it's completely outside the box like a dream board, YouTube video or web page. A most important aspect of this practice is to have fun.

C H A P T E R T E N

Real-Life Conscious Businesses
Doing Well by Doing Good

Principles of new ways of doing business are great, but I wanted to see if there were companies out there who are actually already doing it... Companies who think it's not only a nice thing or a PR campaign to "do well by doing good," but who actually see it as a core purpose, mission, founding principle or culture of their company. And then we wanted to talk to them to get their story.

The hunt began. My crack research team of Heather Swick and J-Coby Wayne and I brainstormed companies or products we knew personally and companies that had been in the news over the years for cool and innovative ways they give back. We looked at the membership list of the Conscious Capitalism Institute, and we studied which companies are B Corporations certified by B Lab.

The Conscious Capitalism Institute (www.cc-institute.com) is a non-profit founded by businesspeople and business academics to be a primary hub of the "conscious capitalism movement" and to share knowledge through research, education and training on conscious business best practices.

B Corporations provide a framework and certification for companies wishing to benefit society as well as their shareholders. As of the publishing of this book, 28 states in the US have put legislation in place to allow B Corps as legal entities. According to the Benefit Corporation Information Center (benefitcorp.net), benefit corporations: 1) have a corporate purpose to create a material positive impact on society and the environment; 2) are required to consider the impact of their decisions not only on shareholders but also on workers, community, and the environment; and 3) are required to make available to the public an annual benefit report that assesses their overall social and environmental performance against a third-party standard.

B Lab (www.bcorporation.net) is a non-profit certifying body, so while not all Benefit Corporations are B Lab-certified, those are the ones we looked for in scouting out conscious businesses to interview and profile for this book. Here's B Lab's B Corporation Declaration of Interdependence to give you an idea of what B Lab is trying to help bring to life as a new business model and structure:

B CORPORATION DECLARATION OF INTERDEPENDENCE

We envision a new sector of the economy

which harnesses the power of enterprise to create public benefit. This sector is comprised of a new type of corporation - the B Corporation - which is purpose-driven, and creates benefit for all stakeholders, not just shareholders.

As members of this emerging sector and as entrepreneurs and investors in B Corporations,

We hold these truths to be self-evident:

That we must be the change we seek in the world.

That all business ought to be conducted as if people and place mattered.

That, through their products, practices and profits, businesses should aspire to do no harm and benefit all.

To do so, requires that we act with the understanding that we are each dependent upon another and thus responsible for each other and future generations.

In the life of business, B Corporations are still relatively new (as of 2015). I actually worked with one of the first B Corps in Houston, Texas in 2006. You can find the B Corp timeline here: www.bcorporation.net/what-are-b-corps/the-non-profit-behind-b-corps/our-history, and FYI, King Arthur - one of our interviewees - was first to use the B Corp Logo. In the spring of 2015, Etsy, a highly popular online marketplace to make, sell and buy goods (many of which are handmade by individuals around the world), got a lot of attention as it was only the second certified B Corporation that went public, and it was definitely the first high-profile, well-known company that happened to be a B Corporation to go public (though most people probably didn't know it was a B Corporation until it announced that it was going public).

Its IPO (initial public offering) stimulated a lot of speculation because a B Corporation's legal mandate and performance measures are currently quite different from a traditional publicly-traded company's (public benefit for the community at large versus profit for a few). Etsy's opening share price indicated that the market had enough curiosity and confidence that Etsy will over time be able to both make money and adhere to its purpose and principles as a certified B Corporation, but there's still much speculation about whether it will be able to get its B Corporation status renewed as a publicly-traded company on the stock market.

While market watchers wait to see what will happen with Etsy, some traditional heavy hitters in the business world have publicly questioned the over-focus on shareholders as a sound strategy in the wake of the 2008 economic contraction. Data show that taking care of your primary direct constituents - employees, customers and your products/services - may be better for the long-term health and growth of your company. Take a look at the chart from Simon Sinek's book, *Leaders Eat Last,* of GE's versus Costco's growth over 30 years. GE prioritized their shareholders. Costco prioritized customers and employees.

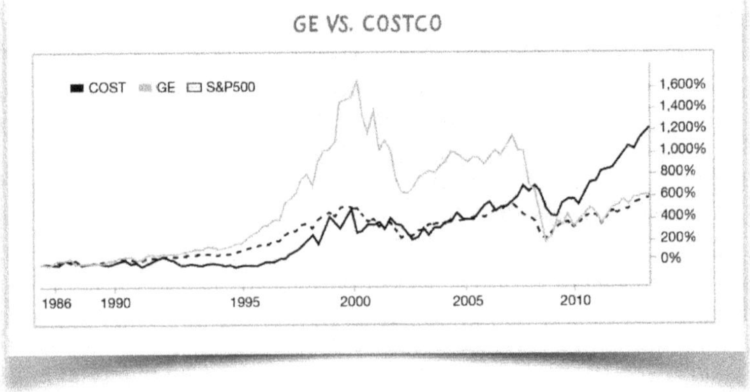

This, of course, is only one case, but in a 2009 interview with Steve Dennings in *Forbes* magazine, GE's long-time past CEO, Jack Welch - known during his tenure for his tough, take-no-prisoners leadership style and focus on shareholders - shared his changed perspective on putting shareholder value above all else as compared to making employees, customers and products the core focus.

> "
>
> *On the face of it, shareholder value is the dumbest idea in the world. Shareholder value is a result, not a strategy... your main constituencies are your employees, your customers and your products. Managers and investors should not set share price increases as their over-arching goal... Short-term profits should be allied with an increase in the long-term value of a company.*
>
> "

Time will tell if Benefit Corporations gain traction as a viable model of conscious business principles and practices.

In searching for conscious businesses to interview and profile in this book, we aimed for a mix of industry/product, size, geographical location and leadership demographics (age, gender and ethnicity). We also wanted to include a few companies we personally believed in because of the products, services or experiences they offer. We think we achieved our goals, and we are happy and proud to bring these companies to your attention as an inspiration to bring this book's 9 principles into your own business, social media and life.

As we were editing this book and wondering about having to get permission to use any of the logos of our profiled companies, we stumbled on Super, a new online community app created by Biz Stone, Twitter's founder. We chose to use their logo as the opening image for this chapter because: 1) they actually encourage people to download their logo on their website, which we thought was a great example of sharing and coming from abundant exchange; and 2) more importantly, their purpose statement and founders' statement are about as conscious as it gets. Since it was too late in the production cycle of this book to interview them, we wanted to make sure they were at least included and that you would get a chance to learn more about them. Here's Super's purpose statement from their website (www.super.me) and their founders' statement:

OUR PURPOSE

INSPIRE EMPATHY

The right composition of images and text can convey more emotion than either images or text alone. Super uses "starters"—like MY FAVORITE or DID YOU KNOW—along with suggested images to make posting in the community fun. It's a new and unique way to connect with people on a deeper level.

Super was founded by Biz Stone and Ben Finkel who both believe a company can do well by doing good, that work should be fun, and that the secret to success is having a healthy work life balance. They are also big fans of battle-tested clichés.

Let's turn now to our profiled companies. Here's who we talked to:

- Blinds.com
- Chandah Space Technologies
- Do Good Real Estate
- Give Something Back
- Green Lite Cafe
- Guayaki
- King Arthur Flour

To profile these companies, we developed our own interview questions and emailed them to the companies, with the offer for us to interview them in person or for them to email back their responses. We ended up getting our interview responses through both methods.

Here is the interview questionnaire we developed:

1. What do you hope to contribute and bring to the world through your business?

2. Would you consider yourself a conscious business doing good? How do you define "a conscious business?"

3. What conscious business practices do you employ? How have these conscious business practices made a difference in your business and/or the community?

4. How did your company become a conscious business? Did you start out that way when it was founded, or did it evolve over time? If over time, how did that happen? What course of events led to your company becoming a

conscious business?

5. Do you have a spiritual philosophy that has guided your company to do good through conscious business practices?

6. What do you see as the role of business in society in general?

7. Do you have any advice for other companies who are trying to create or evolve into a conscious business?

Here's how our profiled companies responded:

BLINDS.COM

COMPANY OVERVIEW

Blinds.com is a Houston, Texas-based company that sells different types of blinds, shades, draperies, valances, shutters, skylights, arches and vertical blind alternatives and offers home decorating trends and do-it-yourself projects for its customers. Blinds.com began in 1986 as "Laura's Draperies" and has expanded over the years to its current company today. One of Blinds.com's core values is to "continuously improve," and Blinds.com believes that improving the community is an essential way to embody that core value every day. Their cultural committee chooses charities throughout the year that they can serve. Some charities that they have contributed to over the years include: The AIDS Foundation Houston, Easter Seals Disability Service, Habitat for Humanity, Habitat for Humanity ReStore, the H.O.M.E Foundation, Houston Foodbank, The Furniture Bank-Houston, March of Dimes, Houston SPCA,

Susan G. Komen For the Cure, Via Colori-The Street Painting Festival, Wounded Warrior project and YMCA Operation-Backpack.

Interview with Jay Steinfeld, Founder & CEO

1. What do you hope to contribute and bring to the world through your business?

I view my business as a platform on which I can achieve my purpose to "help people become better than they ever believed possible." At Blinds.com, I've been able to do this by fostering a company culture that encourages (really, requires!) living our company's 4 Core Values:

1. Improve continuously
2. Experiment without fear of failure
3. Be yourself and speak up
4. Enjoy the ride!

These core company values are powerful and provide a framework to make important business decisions and guide us during our intensive hiring process. Considering the amount of time we spend in the workplace, I strongly believe that creating a working environment that demands continuous growth and excellence will have a positive impact person by person and on the world at large.

2. Would you consider yourself a conscious business doing good? How do you define "a conscious business?"

I don't define a business as good or conscious, but I do define people that way. Creating a business culture that supports employees on their journey of improvement and empowerment means playing an important role in helping people be and do good.

I've had more than a few employees share personal stories with me about how their experience working at Blinds.com has dramatically impacted their personal lives. When you open the door in someone's mind that they can grow themselves into whatever they truly want to be and that their ideas are valuable and worth sharing - that empowerment doesn't stop as they leave the office building. It continues on into their relationships at home and in the way they act in their lives from every angle.

This is a great way for the people that make up a business to "do good" - define success as growing the people around you into their optimal selves that do great things in the world around them.

3. What conscious business practices do you employ? How have these conscious business practices made a difference in your business and/or the community?

I'm not sure how to answer this as I don't define ethical, human-sensitive behaviors as business practices, but more as a mindset.

4. How did your company become a conscious business? Did you start out that way when it was founded, or did it evolve over time? If over time, how did that happen? What course of events led to your company becoming a conscious business?

I have evolved as a person over the years, so it makes sense that my business would see a similar change. My personal moment of clarity, which had an enormous impact on Blinds.com, occurred after the death of my wife, Naomi, and after months of serious introspection. I was on an Alaskan cruise ship, trying to find some meaning during a very challenging time in my personal life when I realized that my personal definition of what it means to be successful needed a dramatic re-vamp.

It was at this point that I realized the true way to be successful was not by accumulating wealth or possessions - or even hitting certain revenue goals in my business - but rather by building up the people around me to help them reach their maximum potential. The success of those around me was to become my own personal success. And that understanding changed everything.

From then on, I worked hard to be less of a micro-manager and more of a success coach to my employees. By focusing on ongoing iterative improvements in both the business and in my employees' personal development, we were able to realize much greater success than by focusing on the bottom line alone.

5. Do you have a spiritual philosophy that has guided your company to do good through conscious business practices?

It's perhaps more of a life philosophy than spiritual - I find it tremendously important for people to not just focus on making themselves better, but to make everyone around them better - including the community.

It's then only natural to give back to the community and to help them too become better. And this is how I define my personal success: to be in the process of improving myself and all others. So this is also how I have defined my success as a CEO - it's my job to make sure that my company reflects that by hiring like-minded employees and providing every opportunity for them to grow and be the very best versions of themselves.

This is also where community participation, volunteering and non-profit fundraising comes into place in the Blinds.com office.

If the evolution of self and others is defined as spiritual, then so be it.

6. What do you see as the role of business in society in general?

I am a strong believer in capitalism and in taking care of your people and customers in whatever way possible. I am proud to provide jobs to over 250 incredible employees and to be a big part of many other vendor companies' success. By providing a positive working environment and generous compensation/benefits, thoughtful companies are growing future community leaders, non-profit volunteers and donors. We are fueling the economy, we are funding college educations and dreams, we are even inspiring employees to leave and start their own businesses (how thrilling!). The role of my business is in providing for my employees' future, in taking exceptional care of our incredible customers and in being the kind of organization that I hope many others can model themselves after.

7. Do you have any advice for other companies who are trying to create or evolve into a conscious business?

Meaning matters. Culture matters. Look deep into your core as a person (not simply as a business owner) and strive to understand yourself first, then find ways that you can organically instill the driving force that motivates your personal life into your business.

The people that you surround yourself with are crucial - not only to your business success, but also to the kind of company culture that begins to grow and impact your employees and customers. You want a wide diversity of employee backgrounds, experiences and talents - but in the same breath, you want to find incredible people that share the same vision, personal drive and passion for life.

(Editor's note: Blinds.com was acquired by The Home Depot as this book was in editing and production.)

CHANDAH SPACE TECHNOLOGIES

COMPANY OVERVIEW

Chandah Space Technologies is a Houston, Texas- and Mountain View, California-based aerospace company working on developing innovative technologies and capabilities in space. They design and build small aircraft. Chandah Space Technologies focuses on small satellites design, development and operations. The vision of Chandah Space Technologies is to transform the economics of doing business in orbit. Their team and partners include marquee aerospace organizations and individuals with deep domain expertise and a passion for space.

Interview with Adil Rahim Jafry, Chairman & CEO

1. What do you hope to contribute and bring to the world through your business?

Better understanding among people of different backgrounds and cultures; better tools (including technologies) to manage future risks for the society as a whole; and help make space exploration sustainable.

2. Would you consider yourself a conscious business doing good? How do you define "a conscious business?"

Yes, I do consider Chandah Space Technologies to be a conscious business doing good. My definition of a "conscious business" would be an organization that evaluates the visible (and potentially invisible) impacts of its decisions holistically and in a manner that creates least harmful future impact of its actions while maximizing the good for the most stake-holders. I also believe that one ought to consider the term over which impact is evaluated over centuries, not just years or decades.

3. What conscious business practices do you employ? How have these conscious business practices made a difference in your business and/or the community?

We foremost require ethical behavior in business practices and are driven by the desire to minimize damage of our products and services on the society as a whole. We have strong governance (Board of Directors and Advisors), and they come from diverse backgrounds. Additionally, we believe that innovation and exploration are the keys to realizing full potential for any organization. In general we put both human beings and the well-being of the ecosystem as a whole at the center of our work. Our strong governance and high ethical standards have enabled us to attract high-quality team members and partners. In turn, this has further catapulted us to the center of innovation in the space industry.

4. How did your company become a conscious business? Did you start out that way when it was founded, or did it evolve over time? If over time,

how did that happen? What course of events led to your company becoming a conscious business?

I believe it was a function of quality individuals and a team with strong vision to do good that allowed us to inculcate this mindset. Further, space requires pristine execution - and there is really very little room to go wrong. Hence we decided to adopt high standards in organizational and personal conduct early on in our inception.

5. Do you have a spiritual philosophy that has guided your company to do good through conscious business practices?

Yes, I believe there is more to ourselves and our lives than what simply meets the eye. For example, often I find myself wondering where, how and why it all began - and don't necessarily find all the explanations provided by detailed study of observable natural phenomena (science) alone to be satisfactory. Hence being mindful of one's actions through conscious decision-making allows one to explore the interconnected nature of reality and, in my opinion, is critical to discovering the meaning of life.

6. What do you see as the role of business in society in general?

To enable individuals who develop arts, crafts, products and services to efficiently exchange their wares for what they need in a high integrity setting.

7. Do you have any advice for other companies who are trying to create or evolve into a conscious business?

Yes - be mindful, do good, and don't take good people and nature for granted.

DO GOOD REAL ESTATE

COMPANY OVERVIEW

Do Good Real Estate is a next-generation boutique Real Estate brokerage company specializing in residential properties throughout Wilmington, North Carolina and Wrightsville Beach, North Carolina. Do Good Real Estate focuses on the core business values of: service, honesty, and treating people right. Do Good Real Estate donates 6% of their total commission from each home they sell to people and places that need it more than they do. Their goal is to create a real estate brokerage that matters.

Interview with John Jackson, Founder & CEO

1. What do you hope to contribute and bring to the world through your business?

That people feel invigorated and find purpose in their work. Before consumers buy a house you want them to feel good about their decision and purchase and have no remorse. I want consumers to feel good working with a company that cares. I hope to "lead by example." There is power in that with companies who are practicing conscious business practices. When things are done correctly (when companies are doing good and practicing abundance), there is money to give back. I hope to bring to the world a sense of "healthy capitalism."

2. Would you consider yourself a conscious business doing good? How do you define "a conscious business?"

Yes, I would consider my business a conscious business doing good. I worked in New York City prior to moving to North Carolina, and I have found that working in a smaller city makes a business and its employees more visible. I would define a "conscious business" as one that pays a living wage, pays local service providers a living wage, is environmentally conscious, thinks where their money is going, and is helping the community. I would go off of the B Corporation definition as well. (See this book's Resources appendix for a link to the B Corporation website.)

3. What conscious business practices do you employ? How have these conscious business practices made a difference in your business and/or the community?

The conscious business practices that we employ are giving back to non-profits, using local vendors, going paperless when applicable, "paying a living wage" - our agents are independent contractors and are compensated with better commission splits than the standard market. Our contractors are paid market value or better. I had to figure out a way for my business to stand out from other real estate businesses, and it made sense to structure this real estate business from the perspective of a company doing good. I don't know if there are other real estate businesses functioning this way.

4. How did your company become a conscious business? Did you start out that way when it was founded, or did it evolve over time? If over time, how did that happen? What course of events led to your company becoming a conscious business?

This business became a conscious business when it was founded. A childhood friend started the business idea, and around 2007/2008 we explored how we could do business better. It is written in our business plan and in legal documentation that this business model (a conscious business/business doing good) will stay enforced.

5. Do you have a spiritual philosophy that has guided your company to do good through conscious business practices?

"In matters of style swim with the current. In matters of principle be like a rock."

6. What do you see as the role of business in society in general?

The role of business should be altruistic in nature. We are all so connected today; I feel we will be more altruistic as we progress. I feel that the role of business should be to provide a good or service or product that moves humanity forward. Businesses are an evolution. We need more "Do Good Real Estates" in the world. We need more trans-parency to come to the market. We need to maintain relationships. All the things that help make businesses connect with consumers and other businesses and the community will make us more wholesome and caring.

7. Do you have any advice for other companies who are trying to create or evolve into a conscious business?

"Be nimble and stay the course." If you have your heart in it, you have to stay the course. Have your heart drive your passion. I would say for business owners to have a good idea and passion behind it and recognize weaknesses as well. Their most important asset is your time. Be honest with yourself and hire or delegate out that which you cannot perform yourself for the business. Tap into the network of people who will help make and build a great company.

GIVE SOMETHING BACK

COMPANY OVERVIEW

Give Something Back is a certified B Corporation member that sells a range of office supplies. Their purpose is to "exist to improve the quality of life in their communities." They do this by serving and delighting their customers, giving time and profits to the community, growing employees and helping them realize their full potential and leading others by inspiring them to give, serve and grow. Their values are focused on integrity, teamwork, diversity, passion and environmental stewardship. Give Something Back's corporate headquarters is located in Oakland, California with Regional Offices in Sacramento, California and San Diego, California.

Interview with Michael Hannigan, President

1. What do you hope to contribute and bring to the world through your business?

Goal: Consistence. Use business as a tool to use profits and give back to non-profit organizations. I also hope to create fair and equal distribution of wealth. Our business is focused on transferring wealth from the company to non-profits and out into the community. We hope to create a community control model of the economy.

2. Would you consider yourself a conscious business doing good? How do you define "a conscious business?"

A "conscious business" is a business that measures and holds themselves accountable to stakeholders and not just investors. A "conscious business" expands their understanding of their actions on the community. A "conscious business" needs to find balance: what is the balance? A business needs to intentionally think about the range of impact that it will have on stakeholders and how to reconcile that impact. Stakeholders need to have an input in what the range of impact will be.

3. What conscious business practices do you employ? How have these conscious business practices made a difference in your business and/or the community?

We employ standard business practices and pay taxes to help build the infrastructure of society. We operate intentionally for other stakeholders, and our employment policies create community value by hiring people who have not had hiring opportunities before. We rise to the level of productivity and make more environmentally-conscious decisions.

Our conscious business practices have made a difference:

- For example, we use a B Corp bank or a local bank so that our financial investments are able to flow back through the community.
- Payroll is determined by the marketplace.
- When our conference rooms are not being used, we extend offers to non-profit companies to be able to use our conference rooms for meetings or events.
- We donate our profits to non-profit organizations.
- We build profits for the community.
- We use our delivery trucks for service. For example, we have our delivery trucks make their stops for the day, and then on their way back to the warehouse (with their empty truck), they pick up electronic waste from other companies and bring that back to the warehouse so that E-Waste Recyclers in California can pick it up.
- Another example is our service work for food banks. Delivery trucks will stop at local grocery

stores and pick up food bins that they will then bring back to our warehouses. Once the delivery trucks bring back a good amount of food bins, local food bank trucks come to the warehouses to pick up the food bins and then they are able to bring them back to their center for distribution. We do this so that it saves the food banks money and to support feeding the local community.

4. How did your company become a conscious business? Did you start out that way when it would founded or did it evolve over time? If over time, how did that happen? What course of events led to your company becoming a conscious business?

This company become a conscious business when it was founded. The company was founded in 1991 and has been in business for 23 years. After I graduated college, I went to work for companies like Xerox where I moved up in ranks and had many executive jobs. About 12 years after school, I learned how to run a business in that environment. I was always interested in community service work. In 1990, I was going through a divorce. And when you get divorced you want to eat reasonably, so I would eat spaghetti. And so I would also buy spaghetti sauce. One day, I was in the grocery store and I noticed "Newman's Own" tomato sauce on the shelf. I read on their label "all profits are donated to charity." I thought to myself that the community will benefit if I buy this sauce. So that is how it started. I was inspired by that, and it demonstrated to me that it was possible to sell products to consumers and then give back to the community. I learned that it was not a crazy idea and there was no sacrifice involved to be successful. And when we started this business it worked right away. It was not a huge risk at all.

5. Do you have a spiritual philosophy that has guided your company to do good through conscious business practices?

No, we do not have a spiritual philosophy that has guided our company. We use skills for the betterment of the community. We operate from a sense of sharing resources and creating fairness in the community. We again go back to wanting to change the way wealth is shared in the community.

6. What do you see as the role of business in society in general?

I see the role of business as providing a community benefit. I see the role of business as supporting the distribution of goods and services to the community. Also, a business needs to be held accountable for how it affects the community. A business needs to contribute value to the community as a whole. The value of life is in the community. Prior, businesses have done well, but the communities have suffered.

7. Do you have any advice for other companies who are trying to create or evolve into a conscious business?

Make sure you know how the business functions. Look into the 28 states that have implemented B Corporation laws and have created legal structure to create value in the community. Look into the institutional permanence behind it now. Create and measure wealth by how it is distributed to the community.

GREEN LITE CAFE & EATERY

COMPANY OVERVIEW

Green Lite Café & Eatery is located in Hamilton, Bermuda and is a family-owned vegan and vegetarian restaurant. Green Lite Café & Eatery provides a broad range of healthy vegan and vegetarian food options as well as a salad and smoothie bar to choose from. Their dishes are filled with love and infused with health. This is displayed in their beautiful food preparation and display of their dishes.

Interview with Shawnette Simmons Smith, Owner-Manager

1. What do you hope to contribute and bring to the world through your business?

What we hope to contribute and bring to the world through our business is twofold. Firstly, through our business we wish to share with the community the fast-growing trend of Healthy Eating. We want to show that choosing healthier options can be truly beneficial to the mind, body and soul. We are not trying to force this new concept on anyone, however we offer it in a way that people can try what we have without wasting the organic and fresh cuisine that we prepare. We also want to offer a place where you can be greeted with pleasant, warm and friendly staff. Where the atmosphere is wholesome and inviting.

2. Would you consider yourself a conscious business doing good? How do you define "a conscious business?"

Yes, we are definitely a conscious business doing good. We define a conscious business as one that has the needs of the people and the environment in mind.

3. What conscious business practices do you employ? How have these conscious business practices made a difference in your business and/or the community?

We work very closely with the community, churches and schools helping with programs and events that are community-based. We offer food services and assistance (whether financial or our physical efforts) to ensure the success of any ventures. We are also looking to start a charity under the name of Green Lite that can help to assist students with furthering their education and also sponsor other community "Giving Back Initiatives." It has made a difference in our business because our customers see that we are willing to help support the community and they, in turn, are not afraid to support our business.

4. How did your company become a conscious business? Did you start out that way when it would founded or did it evolve over time? If over time, how did that happen? What course of events led to your company becoming a conscious business?

The company started out as a conscious business. We have lived a life of "All Things In Common" for over 20 years and with that thinking, we look at ways of trying to spread and share what we have with others.

5. Do you have a spiritual philosophy that has guided your company to do good through conscious business practices?

Yes, we do. We started our business based on our spiritual beliefs and principles. They encompass prayer, doing good to others, always invoking positive energy and a good physical and mental being.

6. What do you see as the role of business in society in general?

We see the role of business in society in general as a way to provide an affordable product to the community.

7. Do you have any advice for other companies who are trying to create or evolve into a conscious business?

The advice that we would offer to other companies who are trying to create or evolve into a conscious business is to always provide a service to the community that will effect a positive change in the community. We would also say that the people are the greatest commodity in any form of business, especially conscious business, so it is important to keep their overall interest in mind.

GUAYAKI

COMPANY OVERVIEW

Guayaki is an organic, fair-trade yerba mate company that aims to prove it can be profitable while operating sustainably. Yerba mate is a drink made from the naturally caffeinated and nourishing leaves of the South American rainforest holly tree. Guayaki is a certified B Corporation member, a member of the American Herbal Products Association, a member of the Non-GMO Project, (KSA) Kosher, and Certified Organic, a member of the Fair Trade Federation and Fair Trade Certified. Guayaki's headquarters is located in Sebastopol, California and touches the lives of hundreds of thousands around the world. They harvest their yerba mate from rainforests in South America. Guayaki offers its customers a selection of yerba mate tea bags, loose-leaf mate tea, gourds and bombillas, Terere glass bottles and accessories and gifts.

Interview with Chris Mann, Chairman of the Gourd and CEO

1. What do you hope to contribute and bring to the world through your business? Why did you become a

B corp?

If you have been to Argentina, you know that mate is a drink shared among people as a symbol of hospitality. Through bringing this drink to the world, we aim to create healthy communities in South America, and in all the communities that we touch and impact wherever Guayaki is located. To be a healthy community you have to have a wealth of ecosystem and diversity, robust forest, indigenous communities, and be an important part of the whole culture. You need the food to thrive, and you need to be able to relate as humans. 200,000 acres of rainforest and 1,000 living wage jobs, utilizing the forest as service, can be an economic driver for reforestation and a livelihood for the community.

Guayaki started in 1996/1997. What we were all about was this mission - stewarding and reinventing rainforests and building culture and communities.

In 2007, the folks that founded the B Corp movement found us and asked us to join and help define what companies like Guayaki are and what they weren't. They also wanted us to help get a good sense of how many businesses there are, that we are not alone, that we all want to get better and work together, share best practices, measure what we are doing, figure out how do we get stronger and where we are strong. We believed in their mission as a B corporation and signed their declaration of interdependence as our pledge to become a B corp.

2. Would you consider yourself a conscious business doing good? How do you define "a conscious business?"

Yes, we are a conscious business. Our main elements of

being a conscious business are that we have a holistic approach to the world, and we don't just look to maximize one aspect of business.

A conscious business is looking at your business as a living entity, and as a living entity, how does it work with all the different elements of the business? How can we build something that is congruent through the whole business? That can only happen if our culture is strong and really clear. Externality (the term in economics) - pollution, social injustice - is not usually part of the traditional business model. We take externalities and internalize them in the business (pay living wages, etc.) Costs are being externalized to the public, then subsidizied through food stamps and public insurance and all those other elements - like Walmart, for example. Internalizing those costs and creating a business model taking all those aspects into account is how we describe a conscious business.

3. What conscious business practices do you employ? How have these conscious business practices made a difference in your business and/or the community?

Growing all products organically, being certified as a fair trade company, B Corp certification, the concept of taking the mate back to where it is natively grown - back to the rainforest - and working with the indigenous communities, who then manage the forest and harvest the mate. This thus creates a virtuous cycle of restoring the forest, creating sustainable income for the community at large.

One way these practices have made a difference is teaching and having indigenous communities learning how to run a business and learning how to balance short-term needs and long-term goals. We help empower communities. We help communities get out of genocide, and then they can build a community, they can survive on the brink of genocide, they can be leaders in their country and in the world. Having this kind of partnership has been a life-changing experience.

Other ways our practices are making a difference in the community: We are touching about 100,000,000 people or more (rough estimate). We have 55 employees, 275 brokers, 500 suppliers, and we are located in 25 different communities across the world with 100,000 plus people in each of those communities. I am also involved in OSC-Squared (One Step Closer to One Sustainable Community) in the Bay Area. It is composed of CEOs in the food industry that are helping each other with projects and of a big industry issues packing coalition, and we are working on biodegradable packaging. We also mentor entrepreneurs and non-profits that are doing good things! A key way to evolve is networking with other like-minded communities; it helps keep you inspired.

4. How did your company become a conscious business? Did you start out that way when it was founded, or did it evolve over time? If over time, how did that happen? What course of events led to your company becoming a conscious business?

We were founded as a conscious business. Every person who has come into Guayaki has come in with alignment to that purpose and has come in as a strong person.

5. Do you have a spiritual philosophy that has guided your company to do good through conscious business practices?

Not one central philosophy, but one underlying theme has been that we are spiritual beings, we are all energy, and we are all here to make the world a better place. That starts with our self, and that ripples out to all businesses and the relationships that we have. How do we become better people? Thinking about that then creates better relationships. The more positive energy we bring, especially when running a business - having that passion and that belief - is really powerful. Another element we believe is that people are inherently good, and people want to be loved and love, and create positive experiences. We believe in trusting in people, and that by building positive relationships, we can trust in people.

According to the *Physician's Desk Reference*, mate's health benefit is that it regulates heartbeat. You are sharing mate out of the same vessel - a gourd. Drinking out of a shared vessel creates a level of connection and communication with others. Mate drinking is supposed to be a slowing down process where you are able to focus and relax. It is a vital part of the whole process.

Mate opens your heart and stimulates sharing in conversation and bonding. It makes you feel energized and alive. Our slogan is: *Come to life!* We mean it in the sense of coming to life and bringing your gifts to life!

6. What do you see as the role of business in society in general?

I see business as a way to organize people to accomplish a service that benefits society. So in some ways talking about mate as a way to steward and restore rainforests creates a society that is growing and improving. I see business as bringing purpose to life rather than doing business as usual. More and more people are recognizing that what I do to make a living is connected to who I am as a person. That creates a description as a person, and people want to be unified, aligning their purpose with their livelihood. It's easier to start a company now than before - it may not be as easy to succeed - but it is easier to find companies to participate in starting a business. Business's role in society in general is to help people find purpose, and the clearer a company is with their purpose, the more likely that company is to attract people to that purpose. It is easier to attract those with the same purpose. In the case of a business, you are generating income that becomes the energy you can compensate people with.

7. Do you have any advice for other companies who are trying to create or evolve into a conscious business?

Get clear with yourself on what drives you and what you are passionate about, and then make sure your business is aligning with that as much as possible. It is a never-ending process; it is a process of constantly staying tuned in to what your purpose and mission are, and using them to make decisions. Then it evolves to a way of living and being. It takes time. As you invest your time and energy in doing it, you attract people who are aligned with your same purpose. People that are attracted to Guayaki are those who create our culture and bring our purpose and mission to life. You will change things that aren't in alignment with your purpose and mission as you go. The B Corp assessment is an excellent way to look at tangible tools of a business. It is a good way to look at things you are or aren't doing in your business. It is a tangible way to make improvements in your business.

KING ARTHUR FLOUR

COMPANY OVERVIEW

King Arthur Flour is America's oldest flour company, founded in Boston in 1790 to provide pure, high-quality flour for residents of the newly formed United States. Today they describe themselves as the nation's premier baking resource, offering everything from top-quality baking products to inspiring educational programs. King Arthur Flour is located in Norwich, Vermont and is a certified B Corporation member. As a certified B Corporation member, King Arthur Flour focuses on four core areas: the environment, employees, products and the community. Their focus on these four areas is "their recipe for success in achieving numerous workplace and product awards, growing their team of passionate, and talented employee-owners, and building meaningful relationships with customers worldwide."

Interview responses prepared by King Arthur Flour's Media Department

1. What do you hope to contribute and bring to the world through your business?

King Arthur Flour's mission is to inspire and support bakers through our high-quality products and educational resources.

2. Would you consider yourself a conscious business doing good? How do you define "a conscious business?"

Yes, King Arthur Flour is a conscious business, and we support our community, the environment and our employee-owners. A conscious business understands that profits are just one part of the equation, and giving back can take many forms and should be part of the company's business model.

3. What conscious business practices do you employ? How have these conscious business practices made a difference in your business and/or the community?

King Arthur Flour has several conscious business practices, but the most prominent include:

- Being 100% employee-owned
- Being a founding B Corp
- Being a member of 1% for the Planet
- Providing a plethora of wellness programs for employee-owners, including flexible work schedule, subsidized CSAs, major discount on products, free exercise classes, free wellness screenings and classes, health initiative incentives (i.e., money to quit smoking), access to bicycles and walking trails to get to different buildings and financial incentives for having a green commute
- Giving all full- and part-time employees 40 paid hours of volunteer time a year

Our employee-owners take pride in the work that they do and are much more engaged because they appreciate how well the company takes care of their well-being. King Arthur Flour has a low turnover rate, and many employees stay for life. By creating a respectful and empowering corporate culture, King Arthur Flour makes it possible for our employees to thrive - both in and outside the workplace.

4. How did your company become a conscious business? Did you start out that way when it was founded, or did it evolve over time? If over time, how did that happen? What course of events led to your company becoming a conscious business?

King Arthur Flour has been in business for 225 years and is America's oldest flour company. The company has always taken pride in being a company that goes above expectations, but by becoming a certified B Corp in 2007, we have taken extra pride in knowing a third party can recognize the good we're doing, and it is not just us saying we do good.

5. Do you have a spiritual philosophy that has guided your company to do good through conscious business practices?

No.

6. What do you see as the role of business in society in general?

Businesses should see themselves as a member of their community.

7. Do you have any advice for other companies who are trying to create or evolve into a conscious business?

Your employees are your best asset.

Shelley: "Many thanks to all of these companies and their stewards who shared their experience and wisdom through the conscious business interview questions."

Shelley's Wrap-Up

I found interviewing and sharing the results of these leading-edge companies inspirational. Business can be done for good and can directly affect the bottom line in so many ways, both financially and with many other benefits as shared in an earlier chapter. A special thanks go out to Heather and J-Coby for the awesome work done to engage these diverse companies and to include them in this book. I am encouraged and energized by these conscious businesses who are actually successfully doing well by doing good, and I hope you are, too!

CHAPTER ELEVEN

Practices and Tools
to
Build and Grow Your Conscious Business

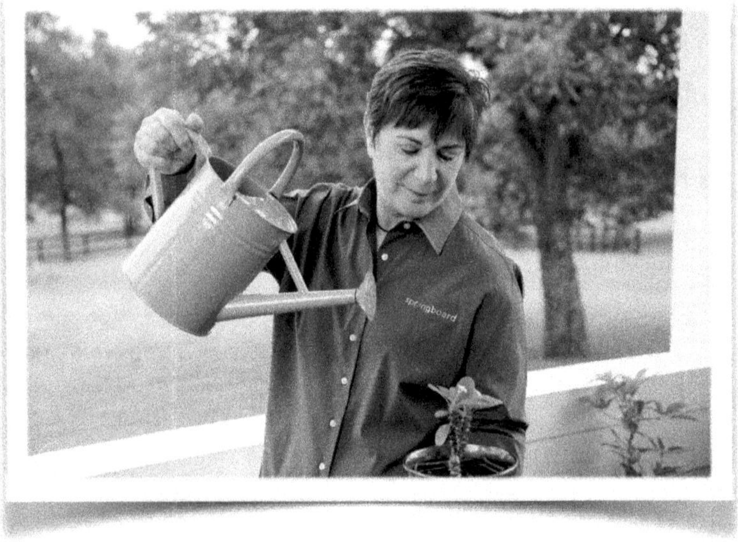

We've explored 9 principles for conscious business, social media and life through my experiences and ideas and the experiences and ideas of our Funday School for Business panelists and audience members.

Now, let's explore some concrete practices and tools you can use to bring the reality of these principles and conscious business into practical action.

TOOL

CHECKLIST TO ASSESS FIT (WITH PROSPECTIVE COMPANIES, PROJECTS, CLIENTS, PARTNERS, ETC.)

How do you currently assess if a company, project, activity, group or work is a fit for you? It's not always easy to figure out if something is a fit for you from the outside - whether it's a job opening or a prospective client or even a prospective non-profit or a cause to support with your company. Fortunately, social media and other online presences like websites and blogs are making it easier than ever to do "due diligence" to see if your values are aligned with the prospective company, project, client, partners, etc. that you are considering.

Here's a checklist:

____ Reviewed the company's mission statement online (or asked them about it), and it contributes to my core values.

____ Reviewed the management team, online and via LinkedIn, to assure a diverse and conscious work force.

____ Reviewed the background of the key players and board members to assure not all are purely sales background.

____ Evaluated the digital footprint of the company, including their business page(s) on Facebook, LinkedIn, etc. to see if there was a "playful" vibe at the company (if playfulness is an important value to you).

____ "Interviewed" the key people that I will be working with/for to determine if they share similar values to mine.

____ Determined that the company gives back to the community in some way, monetarily or time-wise.

____ Determined the company gives people ample opportunity to contribute to good outside the company.

____ Determined the company supports a healthy work force (i.e., provides incentives for the employees to continuously learn/grow/work out, etc.)

____ Determined the company incents employees for volunteering inside of company hours.

TOOL

A CONSCIOUS PROGRESS CHECK WORKSHEET

Conscious businesses don't have much to do with traditional "performance reviews." As we've mentioned throughout this book, it's less about doing than about being. It's less about measuring only profit than about bringing a purposeful culture to life. It's about exploring and developing non-traditional, meaningful measurements of purpose, impact and progress.

Here's a proposed progress check worksheet. It incorporates many of the values and concepts we've shared throughout the book. You could explore using this monthly, quarterly and/or annually to chart how you're doing at bringing conscious business principles, values and practices to life. If you are a solopreneur, try filling it out for yourself with a rhythm that is useful to you and your particular business or project.

1. ***What do you consider the most important principles or values to you in life and work (e.g., honesty, trustworthiness, integrity, high achievement and excellence, opportunities to share ideas and contribute, recognition, independence, self-directed, routine and structure, efficiency, unstructured, adventurous/youthful/playful, etc.)?***

Write down each principle/value that is highly important to you and that you feel defines you as a person and professional.

____

____

____

____

____

____

2. ***Rate from 1-5 (with 1 being not at all and 5 being very much) how much you think the company you work with (or run if you are the leader or a solopreneur) values and supports as part of its culture and practices each value/principle you identified above as very important to you.***

Where ratings are very high or very low, note specific ways in which the company does or does not support that value.

PRINCIPLE/VALUE RATING

___________________________ __________

NOTES

PRINCIPLE/VALUE RATING

NOTES

PRINCIPLE/VALUE RATING

NOTES

PRINCIPLE/VALUE RATING

NOTES

PRINCIPLE/VALUE RATING

______________________________ __________

NOTES

____

____

PRINCIPLE/VALUE RATING

______________________________ __________

NOTES

____

____

3. ***If there are more lower ratings than higher ratings, what can you do to bring your values and the company's values more in alignment?***

Note down specific ideas.

____

____

____

____

____

____

4. If you do not feel there is anything you can do to bring the values more in alignment, what will you do to find other opportunities to be in an environment where the values are more aligned (e.g., with outside groups or interests, by changing jobs, by starting your own project or company)?

Include a schedule or target date(s) for taking action.

____

____

____

____

____

____

PRACTICE

This practice starts stimulating you to consciously think about and craft your company or work as a "conscious business" that is not just bringing good during business hours or as a company, but as a life in the community and world, at all times and in all areas of life.

"Do all the good you can, by all the means you can, in all the ways you can, in all the places you can, at all the times you can, to all the people you can, as long as you ever can."
- John Wesley, 18th century English theologian

List ways you can apply this quote as part of the culture of all aspects of your business.

PRACTICE

This practice gets you thinking about "good" and "love" as assets. Imagine these as line items on a balance sheet.

What would it mean in your business if you considered "good" and "love" as assets or currencies?

How might these assets cause you to do things differently? List concrete examples.

____

____

____

What unique ways can you bring good and love to your employees, customers, your product or service, the community...?

____

____

____

PRACTICE

This practice helps you see the big picture of your company and lifts you up above the details so you can think about the longer-term and wider impact of what your company is bringing to the world, not just in terms of your goods and services, but also as a life in the community and world.

If your company were to disappear today, how would you want it to be remembered? What legacy do you want to create with your business?

PRACTICE

This practice helps you envision what a conscious business practice looks like and how it can be applied, tracked and measured in your company.

How do the following stakeholders experience principle X through your business? Think of what practical form the principle takes for each of the stakeholders below.

Fill in one of the principles from Chapters 1-9 this book or one of your own choosing:

How does your leadership experience this principle through your business?

your investors/partners?

____

____

____

your employees?

____

____

____

your customers?

____

____

____

your suppliers?

____

____

____

your community?

____

____

____

TOOL

A CONSCIOUS BENEFITS/ASSETS CHECKLIST

This practice helps you start thinking outside the box in terms of what's really effective and needed to support your company's health, well-being, happiness, creativity, innovation and productivity.

Conscious businesses go beyond normal business by offering unconventional benefits and services to their leadership, employees and customer communities to support creativity, innovation, relationship-building, collaboration and productivity.

Check off all those that you currently offer or would like to offer:

- Company-paid community service/volunteer work opportunities ______
- Company matching donations for employee volunteer service hours ______
- Company-paid adventure/travel time ______
- Employee-led and -organized adventure/educational trips related to your business' field for the general community/public (e.g., employees at a video production company organizing and leading videography trips to cool places for the general public) ______
- YouTube channels where customers/users can share what they've created using your product or service (see GoPro Channel on YouTube for example) ______

- Company-sponsored or -organized time in nature ______
- Sleep/nap spots in the office ______
- Outdoor work/thinking spaces at the office ______
- Company-provided alternative transportation (e.g., bikes) ______
- Standing desks ______
- Collaborative work spaces ______
- Concrete ways that encourage cross-departmental cooperation and problem-solving ______

  List specific ways:

  ____

  ____

  ____

  ____

  ____

- Mentoring ______
- Anonymous idea boxes throughout the workspace and/or online ______
- Games and sanctioned play time/ game time at the office (e.g., volleyball courts, intramural sports teams, board games) ______
- In-person and/or online social interaction events at the office or among colleagues (e.g., pizza parties, trivia nights) ______
- Music space at the office with instruments, listening equipment and recording equipment with

opportunities for employees to share music they have created in the space ______

- Art space at the office with art supplies and inspiring artwork on the walls with opportunities for employees to share artwork they have created in the space ______
- Library/reading room at the office with books from many fields, not only related to the company's field, to stimulate genius thinking of connecting the dots from many creative stimuli ______
- Use of unconventional work modes measured and rewarded in annual reviews (e.g., adventure trips taken, nap time used, volunteer work hours, participating in games and social events, collaboration with other departments, mentoring, etc.) ______

PRACTICE

This practice helps you understand how your company or business is perceived and sparks you to think creatively about what kind of "vibe" or culture you want to create to be known as a conscious business.

Use social media, email or in-person survey to ask your:

leadership
investors
employees
customers
vendors/suppliers
community

to describe the vibe or culture of your company, service or product in one word.

What one word would YOU like to use to describe the vibe or culture of your business?

____

PRACTICE

This exercise helps create collaboration, inclusiveness and a sense of positive engagement throughout your whole organization by getting your employee or colleague input.

Use social media, email or in-person survey to ask your employees or colleagues to share what they think the purpose, vision and mission of your company, service or product is or should be.

Implementing any or all of these practices and tools is a conscious way to build, catalyze and grow your business, social media presence and life. Start today and grow from there. And please do share with me on my social media platforms (access all at www.shelleyroth.com) how you see a shift occurring in your business and life! A first step is all it takes to move forward. Just do it!

CHAPTER TWELVE

Forward into the Future

Using the 9 Principles in Social Media

What's next for me is taking these 9 conscious business principles and practices that I have been living through most of my business life and sharing through the Funday School Hangouts and this book and bringing them to companies ready for the next level of progressive thinking. I have been doing social media for a quite some time, and I really believe that one of the reasons Funday School came into being was to bring this book and the accompanying workshops and seminars into businesses ready for some "new age" thinking. I have resisted working with big companies due to my personal experiences in corporate sales even though I was wildly successful, but it is time for me to get out of my own way and be open to bringing Funday School principles to businesses that I resonate with and that resonate with me.

The Funday School Hangouts were really about new philosophies and putting the 9 principles into practice to change your business and your life. Everything in nature is ebb and flow - birth, death and regeneration. Take the time to reflect. Don't feel guilty that you are not being productive in the way that productivity has been traditionally defined. That "nonproductive" time is really about productivity. It is a regeneration of your energy, your muse, and a way for you to commune with nature and realize what's important in your life. That sounds pretty productive to me, yet it seems as human doings we are so concerned with constant motion that we forget to just be. "Shelley Time" is a recurring event on my calendar. Every Monday and Friday is designated "Shelley Time." I don't always get to implement it, but that Shelley Time is really important for me and my business to be successful in meaningful ways that I value.

In doing Funday School and authoring this book, I knew we needed a new balance sheet, a balance sheet measuring other assets as measures of success: measuring how we embrace our conscious-ness and our quality of life, measuring other indicators of "growth" and "health" and "contribution" and "abundant exchange" for our shareholders besides profits.

Funday School for Business will live on and thrive in our workshops, seminars and talks, and all of our panelists are going to be a part of that as well as everybody who has joined in the discussions online. I appreciate all of them being a part of Funday School so much. I appreciate everybody who has watched and continues to watch the video recordings and will attend the workshops, seminars and talks. All the Funday Schools are archived and will continue to be available for viewing on YouTube and LinkedIn via www.shelleyroth.com.

Funday School and this book wouldn't have been possible without social media - from the technology itself of Google Hangouts and internet connectivity to the panelists and audience, many of whom I met via social media, to the 9 principles themselves, which have become so much more real and possible due to the way social media operates. Social media is a great place to put the principles we shared in Funday School into practice. With social media, it's very easy to be a giving, heart-based businessperson, without a primary concern for monetary gain. Not that we don't need to make money of course, but it's an amazing place to come and share from abundance, and with giving, you will grow abundantly. With abundant exchange and fair exchange, there WILL inevitably be an exchange at some point, an exchange of whatever might be needed by that business or individual. It's the law of reciprocity! It's Newton's Third Law of Motion - *for every action, there is an equal and opposite reaction*!

Social media is a fantastic platform for being relevant, but not in a traditional business sense of being relevant, which has tended to be defined as something being used for making money directly, for the typical fashion of selling and marketing and for generating those traditional assets business has typically used to measure success via profit. In using social media in "irrelevant" ways as seen through a traditional and increasingly obsolete lens, I and others using social media in truly giving-to-grow, relationship-based ways are becoming more relevant.

So, how can we use this book's 9 principles in social media?

Principle 1: Give to Grow

This is probably the easiest one since with social media, you can provide any media to share knowledge, humor, discussion and growth - whether you are doing video recordings like I do and providing educational tips; or doing a podcast and recording an audio file to be shared; or posting pictures, memes, quotes to engage with people, bring lightness to their day, meaning in the moment or humor just for the sake of laughter.

Providing online support via your LinkedIn group or Facebook page or other platforms is another example of give to grow. How much fun I have had just giving, without concern for the bottom line and making money. Heck, I don't even look at statistics on Google or other platforms. I have faith that the people that need what I give are getting what I serve up. Numbers are great - and don't get me wrong - as a businessperson, I do believe you need to measure... I just believe that wouldn't it be great if we did more than just measure numbers? Wouldn't it be great if we just KNEW that what we are doing is working because we are living from our purpose and giving to grow... and the rest takes care of itself!! FAITH!

Principle 2: From Return on Investment to Return on Influence

Social media has opened up a world where our social currency defines our ROI, Return on Influence. It is so refreshing to see a level playing field amongst small businesses, as they can have a voice and an easier time of being that true, authentic voice than some of the large corporations. You can create your influence by providing content to others and "giving to grow." You can build an amazing amount of influence and value by contributing to groups on LinkedIn and Facebook, providing comments and support on all social platforms, and even raising awareness for causes and beliefs, all while affecting your ROI.

It can be challenging to measure the ROI of social media. However, if we redefine the meaning of ROI to Return on Influence, then we let go of worrying about profits and being driven purely by profits, and we start considering others before ourselves, building an ongoing network of solid relationships where money is not the motivator, and the engagement, acknowledgement and interaction are all just rewards.

Principle 3: From Scarcity to Abundance

Bringing this principle into action on various social media channels is easy technically, but sometimes still hard attitude-wise. Networks like LinkedIn, Facebook and others make it so easy to "share." When you find a blog or podcast or video or social media post and think to yourself, "Wow, this colleague (old term is competitor) of mine did a great job explaining this or making me laugh or engaging me. Why don't I just share this with my social network?" And, inevitably, many of us may be hesitant to do this. The "scarcity" mentality kicks in and says, "Why would I share a competitor's stuff? I may lose business to this person!"

However, the moment you realize there is more than enough for everyone is the moment you will attract abundance! Being the former sales shark that I was before social media, this was a tough principle to implement, yet, it's so very easy on social media. Now, when I find a colleague that has done a great job on a video or in a blog post, I share that with my network. I know that the people that are supposed to work with me will be attracted to me and those that are not, well, they may go to the colleague for help or they may come to me. In the end, coming from a place of abundance is so much more attractive than coming from scarcity. Give it a go, and see just how you and your business will grow! There is plenty for everyone!

Principle 4: From Competition to Collaboration

Reflecting on my past years in corporate America, it was all about competition, both internally (sales people pitted against each other inside the company) and externally (aiming to win business against competitors at all costs, even when it was not the right solution for the customer). The beauty of social media is we have an opportunity to use our networks to collaborate online with colleagues. I know two brains are always better than one, so using Google Hangouts, for example, can bring together like-minded companies to share ideas and create for the betterment of all.

Social media also helps us realize we may not be the best fit for a certain project, and why not collaborate with someone who brings needed strengths to the relationships you are building in your business? It's easier than ever to find these types of collaborators with social media, but it requires trust and humility and a little bit of letting go of control, which isn't always easy for entrepreneurs or solopreneurs! I encourage you to give it a go. As I've discovered through my own experience, you will experience a whole different level and richness of abundance, inspiration and contribution when you experiment with coming from a collaborative heart rather compared to a mind in competition mode.

Principle 5: From Business as Product to Business as Purpose

While reviewing edits on this book, I came across a young guy who posted an article in a LinkedIn group. The post really excited me about the future of business, and I can't think of a better example of how social media is supporting the shift from business as product to business as purpose.

This young man, David Tunnah, is in transition in his career, and he starts his article off with, "everybody loves to have a strategy." I would add that everybody loves to have a product, something tangible to sell. David shares how having strategy failed him. After two years trying to work his strategy and his plan, he started questioning why he was having struggles even with the strategy in place. He discovered that he couldn't think his way out of the issues he was facing in his business. This led him to understand that you can think your way through life or you can "be" your way through life.

Many of us are taught that being book smart and "mind smart" should be our highest goals. But David actually found that thinking was producing undesirable results. Like many professionals - including me when I was in sales - this thinking and doing approach was making him stressed, anxious and depressed. But he never arrived at the destination he was hoping to reach and hoping that all this misery would eventually deliver.

When things fell apart to the point that he had no resources to fix them, it forced him to try something else: just being himself. Our panelist and this book's editor, J-Coby Wayne, experienced the exact same process in her own career and journey to becoming a better human being, and she has shared a lot with me through her energy guidance about the importance of being and being in the flow of natural rhythms and windows of inspiration rather than trying to push things according to fixed schedules or ideas of how to be productive. The result for me has been much greater abundance and happiness in my business and a release that comes from not always doing. In fact, this book has happened much more slowly than my others because I'm listening much more to how it wants to flow in bringing about a whole new way of "doing business" which isn't about doing at all.

Living the principle of "from business as product to business as purpose," David found that if he gave up his fixed way of being, he opened up many new possibilities that he might not have experienced had he been stuck on business as product versus business as purpose. When he found himself in an empty space of not working, he says he found himself tying to see who he could "call or coax into giving [him] employment," but he ended up having the sense that this was a manipulative act of strategizing to cover up the fact that he was feeling alone, scared and useless. When he realized this, he opened up into feeling and trusting himself to be genuine and honest in sharing his intentions and trusting others. LinkedIn has given him a platform to share his story and for people like me who are active in social media to find him. If you'd like to read the full text of his article, you'll find a link to it in the Resources appendix at the end of this book.

Principle 6: From Profits to Principles

The most obvious way this principle is working in the world of social media and business are the many blogs, images, podcasts, videos and other sources of communication that flow freely. The exchange of information is just incredibly dynamic, and it seems it's about sharing without concern for a return. In addition, social media is being used as a platform for providing customer service above and beyond the traditional phone support we have known in the past. For example, four companies have been noted as standouts for using Twitter effectively to respond to customer complaints:

- **JetBlue** is noted for extremely fast, real-time, sympathetic communications with grounded or flight-delayed customers. Here's an exchange JetBlue had with a disgruntled flyer via Twitter:

Ryan Michael Lazo @RMLazo13 2h
Nothing better than having a delayed flight. Sarcasm at it's finest. Please get me home soon, #jetBlue
Details
JetBlue Airways @JetBlue 1h
jetBlue
@RMLazo13 Please send us your flight number and we'll try to get an update for you.
Details
Ryan Michael Lazo
@RMLazo13
Follow
@JetBlue The flight No. Is 2201. I believe the plane is still in New York as we speak.
Reply Retweet Favorite More
9:09 AM - 1 Jul 13
Reply to @RMLazo13 @JetBlue
JetBlue Airways @JetBlue 1h
jetBlue
@RMLazo13 Your flight is currently scheduled to leave at 11 am. Hang in there. We'll have you on your way as soon as possible.
Details

- **Nike** is noted for being a great example of a huge company making it very easy for customers to interact via social media. It has done this by designating a Twitter account just to respond to customers who need help with anything, @NikeSupport. And people are using it. As of June 2015, @NikeSupport had Tweeted over 402,000 times, as compared to only 19,600 times at their general Nike handle account.

- **Seamless**, an online food delivery service is noted for its round-the-clock customer service across multiple time zones since it offers food delivery all throughout the United States and in London. With social media, companies have increasing opportunities to offer 24-hour customer service (but it also means you have to build into your business and social media strategy how you will respond in a timely manner when even you are sleeping!).

- Cable TV companies aren't always known for their superlative customer service, but **Comcast** is another one like JetBlue that is using Twitter to be able to interact with customers remotely and in real time, including being able to troubleshoot quickly. Responding fast with accurate technical information and a genuine effort to help, especially when it comes to technology, can create a happy warm and fuzzy feeling for your customers, which results in a more engaged community of fans, not just customers or users. Here's an example of an exchange with a frustrated customer who actually used "#evil" in her Tweet to Comcast (which could have been a real PR disaster if Comcast didn't respond well and helpfully):

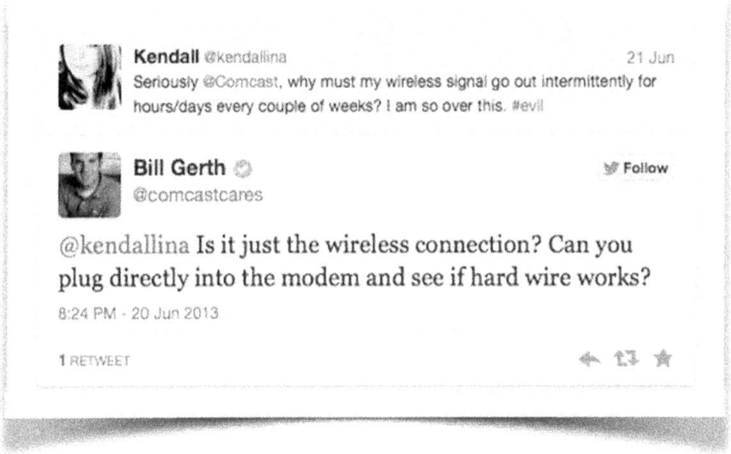

Kendall @kendallina 21 Jun
Seriously @Comcast, why must my wireless signal go out intermittently for hours/days every couple of weeks? I am so over this. #evil
Bill Gerth
@comcastcares
Follow
@kendallina Is it just the wireless connection? Can you plug directly into the modem and see if hard wire works?
8:24 PM - 20 Jun 2013
1 RETWEET

Whether you are sharing knowledge freely or supporting your customer base and others online, coming from integrity and principles rather than worrying about profits is alive and well on social media.

Principle 7: From Productivity to Presence

When I teach my classes, I always make the point that people want to know you. They want to experience you. Sharing pieces of yourself - whether being on the beach in Galveston or traveling to New York City... the whole intention of social media is to be social. To give us an opportunity to share our authentic selves outside of our productive selves as defined by business.

When I scour social media posts, I find that the most engaging ones are about something that speaks to the heart or shared experiences or human interest stories or posts versus business-related posts on Facebook in particular.

Social media helps us discover ourselves and our communities - our "peeps" - through being able to post our interests and how people respond to them. This tells us it's okay to be ourselves, helps us define who our selves truly are, connects us to people who share our interests and loves and gives us permission to bring an expanded, truer, more authentic self to business and life. It truly moves us beyond traditional definitions of productivity to presence where productivity is actually expanded and made more effective because we're not seeing it as productivity or having to be productive; we are taking pleasure and joy in being ourselves and sharing that with others. This is one of the greatest fuels of "productivity" imaginable, and we'll probably see over time that businesses that recognize and nurture this through their culture and structures for employees will be some of the most successful businesses out there.

Principle 8: Bringing Your Purpose and Principles Into Plans and Projects

Social media gives both an external structure and feedback to bring purpose and principles into plans and projects. This is especially important for solopreneurs and entrepreneurs who may be used to stimulation and deadlines set by a corporate setting before they go out on their own. With social media, it presents both the opportunity and the responsibility to be in contact. It sets up a relationship based on sharing value. Content is valuable in social media; it's the main currency.

With social media, you can send out email newsletters once a month. You can write blog posts every few weeks or monthly. You can share a thought-provoking trend or interest to your community weekly. You should be in touch with your social media communities frequently, just as you would be with a friend to maintain a healthy and meaningful relationship. This contact doesn't have to be - in fact, it SHOULDN'T be - all about business or your product or service. It can be a joke or a link to a fun factoid, an amazing video or a cause that's doing good and asking for donations. It can be an update on a big event like the Triple Crown being won for the first time in 37 years or who has won the Academy Awards or the MTV Music Awards if you're serving a younger crowd.

Here's a great example of non-business-specific engagement, a video of an amazing young American Sign Language interpreter interpreting Eminem's rap song, "Lose Yourself", that went viral via YouTube and showed up everywhere on social media while we were editing this book. It's a great example because it raises awareness about Sign Language and hearing issues while being hip to current music and showcasing the accomplishments and creativity of today's youth. See the complete video online at https://www.youtube.com/watch?v=fnAofkVHZOQ.

If you are in communication with your peeps and community via social media, they will give you feedback on the best frequencies to share content and be in touch based on how they like or share or re-post or re-Tweet what you are sharing. You'll also get a sense of what types of content they respond to more than others. You may love sharing philosophical information or new data about trends or technology in your field, but if more people are liking your photo of you and your dog on the beach than your industry-specific info, you know it makes sense to share more of your personal interests and less of your business specifics. This is all great feedback that helps you translate your purpose into specific plans and projects via posting, sharing and emailing.

If your purpose is to help people, then creating a blog, video blog, a "scope" via www.periscope.com or an email marketing newsletter and sharing it on social media are examples of how you can bring your purpose into being; it helps to create a social media production calendar. If your purpose is to educate, social media is a tremendous avenue to deliver that education integrated with your other offerings such as in-person workshops, whether you are posting to a LinkedIn group or writing a blog or responding to questions by people seeking answers from authorities in your field. If your purpose is to provide customer service, what an amazing opportunity to listen to your audience through social media like Twitter and others! If your purpose is philanthropy, there are many sites for giving financial support and donating. Each of the social media platforms provides search tools, so invest a little time in exploring what's out there in the way of groups, pages and communities that you can join and start engaging with.

Principle 9: Reinventing Company Assets

Less than 10 years ago, we couldn't even imagine the future that social media would bring as a voice for employees, customers, company owners. With that voice has come people questioning traditional business-as-usual modes of operation, and entire new "marketing platforms" have been created. Companies have had to start listening to their customers, their employees, their prospects and the community and what THEY value over and above profits. Now, fast-forward almost a decade, and the conversation is out there on: What are corporate assets? What should we be measuring? How can we contribute to the greater good? How can we truly make a difference in the world and still be a profitable company?

It's very apparent with certain companies like Zappos, REI and JetBlue that they are using social media to make a difference, and they're listening to what their stakeholders want. It goes beyond profits and opens up new measurements for company assets such as allowing your employees to bring their dogs to work, which a Central Michigan University study showed contributes to more trust between co-workers and leads to more collaboration among team members. It also gives your company some great pictures and videos to share on social media.

This, in turn, gives your company exposure without having to have a fixed and formal strategy and without having to think so much in terms of direct return on investment. It gives your company the opportunity to just do something because it's fun. This shares out into the community a company culture that cares, that brings a personal element to "business" and that provides an environment that is a great place to work. And because of that, customers are inspired to buy from you and become part of your community because of the principles and ways of being and doing that you're sharing in social media as part of your culture.

Since dogs have been shown to bring so much goodness and happiness to life, and my Corgi dog, Buddy, is one of my greatest inspirations for being instead of only doing and for being present, I can't think of a much happier way to end this book than by sharing the 10 places that allow employees to bring their dogs to work and photos of some of their dogs.

The companies are:

- Replacements, Ltd
- Google

- P & G Pet Care
- Ben & Jerry's
- Autodesk
- Build-A-Bear Workshop
- Klutz; Humane Society
- Amazon
- CLIF Bar

If you'd like to see all the great photos of dogs at work and read the full article, we've provided the link in the Resources appendix at the end of this book. Here are three of the photos from the article:

Klutz

Ben & Jerry's

Google (Photo Credit: FlimSniper/Flickr)

Buddy as a pup, my friend and VP of Morale

I hope you have enjoyed and had as much fun exploring our Funday School for Business 9 principles with me and with our great panelists and Funday participants as we did. I also hope that we've planted the seeds for your business, projects and life to blossom into new ways of bringing consciousness and good into the world! I look forward to seeing you on social media. Please share with me, via www.shelleyroth.com, your stories of applying these principles and how they help your conscious business grow as you travel the path forward.

A P P E N D I X I

Resources
and
References

Here are additional resources to help you explore Give to Grow and the 9 principles further:

B Corporation Information Network
benefitcorp.net

B Lab
bcorporation.net

How to set up co-ops
https://www.sba.gov/content/cooperative

How to set up an ESOP (employee stock ownership plan)
https://www.nceo.org/articles/setting-up-esop

Conscious Capitalism Institute
http://www.cc-institute.com

Video: Why we need to rethink capitalism | Paul Tudor Jones II
https://www.ted.com/talks/paul_tudor_jones_ii_why_we_need_to_rethink_capitalism?language=en

Full Text Transcript: Why we need to rethink capitalism: full transcript | Paul Tudor Jones II
https://www.ted.com/talks/paul_tudor_jones_ii_why_we_need_to_rethink_capitalism/transcript?language=en

...

0:00
This is a story about capitalism. It's a system I love because of the successes and opportunities it's afforded me and millions of others.

0:22
I started in my 20s trading commodities, cotton in particular, in the pits, and if there was ever a free market free-for-all, this was it, where men wearing ties but acting like gladiators fought literally and physically for a profit.

0:40
Fortunately, I was good enough that by the time I was 30, I was able to move into the upstairs world of money management, where I spent the next three decades as a global macro trader. And over that time, I've seen a lot of crazy things in the markets, and I've traded a lot of crazy manias. And unfortunately, I'm sad to report that right now we might be in the grips of one of the most disastrous, certainly of my career, and one consistent takeaway is manias never end well.

1:11
Now, over the past 50 years, we as a society have come to view our companies and corporations in a very narrow, almost monomaniacal fashion with regard to how we value them, and we have put so much emphasis on profits, on short-term quarterly earnings and share prices, at the exclusion of all else. It's like we've ripped the humanity out of our companies. Now, we don't do that - conveniently reduce something to a set of numbers that you can play with like Lego toys - we don't do that in our individual life. We don't treat somebody or value them based on their monthly income or their credit score, but we have this double standard when it comes to the way that we value our businesses, and you know what? It's threatening the very underpinnings of our society. And here's how you'll see.

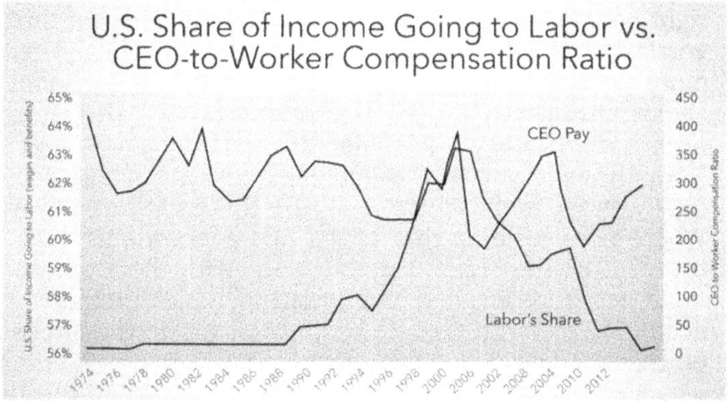

2:10
This chart is corporate profit margins going back 40 years as a percentage of revenues, and you can see that we're at a 40-year high of 12.5 percent. Now, hooray if you're a shareholder, but if you're the other side of that, and you're the average American worker, then you can see it's not such a good thing. ("U.S. Share of Income Going to Labor vs. CEO-to-Worker Compensation Ratio")

2:36
Now, higher profit margins do not increase societal wealth. What they actually do is they exacerbate income inequality, and that's not a good thing. But intuitively, that makes sense, right? Because if the top 10 percent of American families own 90 percent of the stocks, as they take a greater share of corporate profits, then there's less wealth left for the rest of society.

3:02
Again, income inequality is not a good thing. This next chart, made by The Equality Trust, shows 21 countries

from Austria to Japan to New Zealand. On the horizontal axis is income inequality. The further to the right you go, the greater the income inequality. On the vertical axis are nine social and health metrics. The more you go up that, the worse the problems are, and those metrics include life expectancy, teenage pregnancy, literacy, social mobility, just to name a few. Now, those of you in the audience who are Americans may wonder, well, where does the United States rank? Where does it lie on that chart? And guess what? We're literally off the chart. Yes, that's us, with the greatest income inequality and the greatest social problems, according to those metrics. (The US is inside the circle on the top right above the chart.)

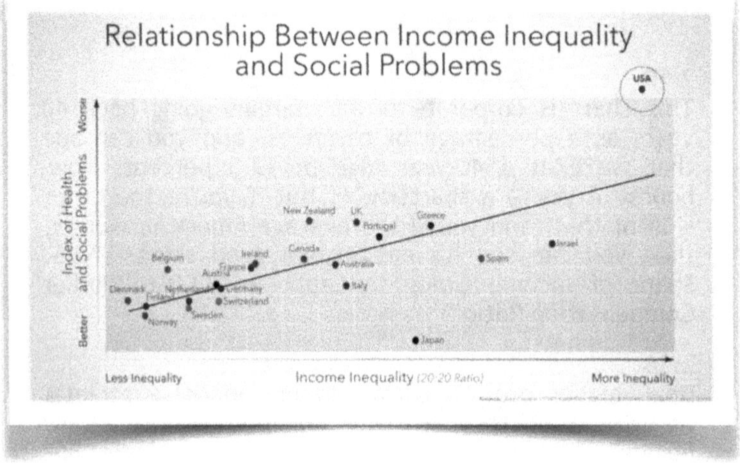

3:53
Now, here's a macro forecast that's easy to make, and that's, that gap between the wealthiest and the poorest, it will get closed. History always does it. It typically happens in one of three ways: either through revolution, higher taxes, or wars. None of those are on my bucket list. (Laughter)

4:15
Now, there's another way to do it, and that's by increasing justness in corporate behavior, but the way that we're operating right now, that would require a tremendous change in behavior, and like an addict trying to kick a habit, the first step is to acknowledge that you have a problem. And let me just say, this profits mania that we're on is so deeply entrenched that we don't even realize how we're harming society. Here's a small but startling example of exactly how we're doing that: this chart shows corporate giving as a percentage of profits, not revenues, over the last 30 years. Juxtapose that to the earlier chart of corporate profit margins, and I ask you, does that feel right?

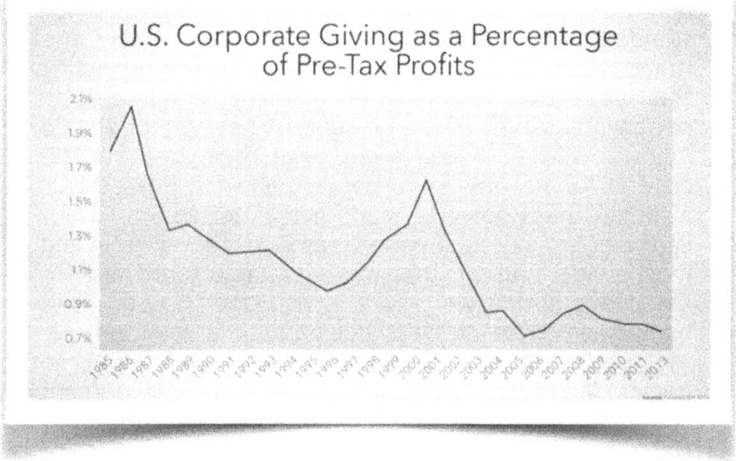

5:07
In all fairness, when I started writing this, I thought, "Oh wow, what does my company, what does Tudor do?" And I realized we give one percent of corporate profits to charity every year. And I'm supposed to be a philanthropist. When I realized that, I literally wanted

to throw up. But the point is, this mania is so deeply entrenched that well-intentioned people like myself don't even realize that we're part of it.

5:38
Now, we're not going to change corporate behavior by simply increasing corporate philanthropy or charitable contributions. And oh, by the way, we've since quadrupled that, but - (Applause) - Please. But we can do it by driving more just behavior. And one way to do it is actually trusting the system that got us here in the first place, and that's the free market system. About a year ago, some friends of mine and I started a not-for-profit called Just Capital. Its mission is very simple: to help companies and corporations learn how to operate in a more just fashion by using the public's input to define exactly what the criteria are for just corporate behavior. Now, right now, there's no widely accepted standard that a company or corporation can follow, and that's where Just Capital comes in, because beginning this year and every year we'll be conducting a nationwide survey of a representative sample of 20,000 Americans to find out exactly what they think are the criteria for justness in corporate behavior. Now, this is a model that's going to start in the United States but can be expanded anywhere around the globe, and maybe we'll find out that the most important thing for the public is that we create living wage jobs, or make healthy products, or help, not harm, the environment. At Just Capital, we don't know, and it's not for us to decide. We're but messengers, but we have 100 percent confidence and faith in the American public to get it right. So we'll release the findings this September for the first time, and then next year, we'll poll again, and we'll take the additive step this time of ranking the 1,000 largest U.S. companies from number one to number 1,000 and everything in between. We're calling it the Just Index, and remember, we're an independent not-for-profit with no bias, and we will be giving the American public a voice. And maybe over time, we'll find out that as people come to know which companies

are the most just, human and economic resources will be driven towards them, and they'll become the most prosperous and help our country be the most prosperous.

8:06
Now, capitalism has been responsible for every major innovation that's made this world a more inspiring and wonderful place to live in. Capitalism has to be based on justice. It has to be, and now more than ever, with economic divisions growing wider every day. It's estimated that 47 percent of American workers can be displaced in the next 20 years. I'm not against progress. I want the driverless car and the jet pack just like everyone else. But I'm pleading for recognition that with increased wealth and profits has to come greater corporate social responsibility.

8:48
"If justice is removed," said Adam Smith, the father of capitalism, "the great, the immense fabric of human society must in a moment crumble into atoms."

9:04
Now, when I was young, and there was a problem, my mama used to always sigh and shake her head and say, "Have mercy, have mercy." Now's not the time for us, for the rest of us to show them mercy. The time is now for us to show them fairness, and we can do that, you and I, by starting where we work, in the businesses that we operate in. And when we put justness on par with profits, we'll get the most wonderful thing in all the world. We'll take back our humanity.

9:42
Thank you.

...

JUSTCapital
justcapital.com

SCORE

score.org

How Zappos CEO Tony Hsieh is bringing new ways of conscious business to Zappos
http://m.fastcompany.com/3044417/zappos-ceo-tony-hsieh-adopt-holacracy-or-leave

Holacracy - a different business strategy model that puts decisions and meaning in the hands of everyone (the model being used by Zappos)
http://www.holocracy.org

"Why I Gave Up Having a Strategy"
https://www.linkedin.com/pulse/why-i-gave-up-having-strategy-david-tunnah

"Personal Purpose - Do You Know What You Want to Be When You Grow Up?"
https://www.linkedin.com/pulse/personal-purpose-do-you-know-what-want-when-grow-up-ian-hacon

"Sense of meaning and purpose in life linked to longer lifespan"
https://www.ucl.ac.uk/news/news-articles/1114/061114-longer-lifespan

Book by Tom Ferguson - *Peerless: Defy Convention, Lead from the Heart, Watch What Happens*
http://www.amazon.com/Peerless-Convention-Heart-Watch-Happens/dp/098949960X/ref=tmm_pap_title_0?ie=UTF8&qid=1403576879&sr=8-1

"This CEO Will Send Your Kids To School, If You Work For His Company"
www.huffingtonpost.com/2015/05/26/boxed-college-tuition-ben_n_7445644.html?ncid=fcbklnkushpmg00000063

"Why This CEO Pays Every Employee $70,000 A Year"
http://time.com/money/3831828/ceo-raise-70000-dan-price/

"4 Examples of Excellent Twitter Customer Service"
http://www.socialmediaexaminer.com/exceptional-customer-service-on-twitter/

Exceptional Young Woman Does Eminem "Lose Yourself" in American Sign Language
https://www.youtube.com/watch?v=fnAofkVHZOQ

"10 companies that let you bring your dog to work"
http://www.mnn.com/family/pets/photos/10-companies-that-let-you-bring-your-dog-to-work/working-like-a-dog

APPENDIX II

About Our Panelists

The Funday School for Business Hangouts and this book wouldn't have been possible without the time and effort of all of our great panelists who lent their experience and insights about giving to grow and the 9 principles explored in this book. So let's learn a little more about them (and about me as the person who brought them all together!).

Isabel Acosta
Network Marketing Professional

I am a network marketing professional. I came into the industry looking to earn some extra money because I was having a hard time making ends meet with my traditional nursing job. And I fell in love with the industry so much that I walked away from my nursing career to do this full time. In this industry of network marketing, it is all about giving to grow. Sales are very much a part of what we do, but it is not selling something to somebody that they don't need. It is us taking the time to find a person that needs our product or needs our business. It very much comes down to getting to know the person before you try to make the sale and listening to their needs to see if you are needed in their lives. A big part of my business is training people how to have their own business and how to meet their financial goals whatever goals they are, whether to make three hundred extra dollars a month or to become financially independent. This is an awesome industry; that's a big reason why I fell in love with it. There are no gaps; there are no limits to what you can achieve. Anybody can do it with whatever education they have, whether it is a high school diploma or a four-year business degree. Once you are in this business, once you dive in, it can be very scary and very overwhelming. As the leader, I have to give to grow. I have to make my team see what is possible. They have to see it through my eyes before they can see it through their eyes.

Website: www.isabel-acosta.com

Lisa Boesen, MAOM, CMC, PHR
Consultant, Speaker, Facilitator, Coach
Live Brilliant, Live Bold, Live Balance
MLC Associates LLC

My passion in life is all about sharing my primary gifts - energy, insight and organization. As a self-proclaimed Domestic Administrator, I am a wife, stepmom, remote caregiver and a small business owner. The title fits all those tasks and small projects I perform to manage the household, save money, improve efficiencies, reduce waste, navigate the healthcare system, garden, maintain a social calendar to improve longevity, nurture friends and family relationships and, of course, make my home pretty. I love: color-coding chaos, Mother Teresa, Warren Buffet, Leonardo DaVinci. My personal mantras are *"In Moderato"* and *"Any more would be too much."*

For those who need a bit more on the professional side, I have over 35 years of experience in healthcare, including clinical management, human resources and performance improvement. I hold a Masters in Organizational Management, and I am a certified master coach, workshop facilitator and compassion fatigue specialist. I love healthcare and enjoy sharing my expertise with consumers and providers alike.

I enjoy working with clients who want to improve personal management skills, navigate change and build resiliency during the cycles of career and life. In addition, I share my experiencing of caring for two parents at the end of life in my book, *Managing the End...to Bridge the Beginning*. I challenge all domestic administrators, both single and partnered, to put PEP (Personal Emergency Preparedness) in their life by using The Domestic Administrator Portfolio.

I enjoy membership and have held leadership positions in multiple healthcare and human resources professional organizations. I have been featured in *Advance Magazine*, *Medical Office Today*, *Mainstreet*, *The Ladders*, *Monster* and *ICU Medicine*.

When not busy color-coding chaos and organizing it into a process flowchart, I sneak off to travel and ride a tandem with my husband to renew, refresh and envision possibilities.

Websites: www.lisaboesen.com,
www.thedomesticadministrator.com

Courtney Coates
Social Media Manager

I have a Graphic Design degree from Louisiana State University. After school, I worked at a design firm in New Orleans until Hurricane Katrina hit and my family and I relocated. Being away from the industry for a few years and away from technology advancements really hindered my opportunity for working again in the graphic design field.

So in 2012 I took my love of graphic design and seized the opportunity to implement it in the new and upcoming social media. My business is expanding monthly, and I now have others that I count on to help me meet my client's needs.

At Co2 Designs, I do social media management. In a nutshell, I post my client's message, content and branding across the social media platforms; send out weekly newsletters; design ads in Photoshop and then post them to Facebook, Google+, Pinterest, Twitter, Yelp, Open Table and Woodlands Online (a local online source).

My biggest business accomplishment has been to double my client base and revenue from last year while cutting back on hours worked, thus allowing me to spend more quality time with my family. Some days, I don't even think of work as "work" as I thoroughly enjoy doing what I do.

Website: www.co2designs2.com

Janet Cohen
Certified Life Coach

I am a certified life coach, and I absolutely love that. Part of my coaching includes writers. I help them get to whatever their writing projects are, and I facilitate some writing groups. I am also a writer myself, and I contract myself out to businesses, small businesses and corporations to write content for them, whether for articles or for my favorite writing, journal writing and creative non-fiction.

Website: www.janetcohen.com

Suzette Cotto
CEO, Innovate Social Media

For over 30 years, Innovate Social Media has been an integral part of building the Internet backbone in over 360 major cities in the US. As founder and CEO, I was responsible for project managing and engineering the first transoceanic internet connectivity from the mainland United States to Hawaii and Mexico.

From building the internet and hosting client servers, I added website design and content management to my company's repertoire in 2007 and studying social media as a business application in 2011.

Innovate Social Media works with companies and sales professionals to develop their knowledge of social platforms as a business networking, prospecting and lead generation tool.

Innovate Social Media also offers the kind of relationship management expertise that keeps sales right on the pulse of buying influencers for business by combining our knowledge of technology and digital strategy development and thus allowing companies to stay "top of mind" with agile response market changes and trends. With consistent and relevant content posting, targeted email communi-cation and telling analytics, Innovate Social Media clients have the edge they need to take business to new levels.

Innovate Social Media is based in Houston, Texas.

Website: www.innovatesocialmedia.com

Sharon Jenkins
Author, Editor, Ghostwriter

I am the Inspirational Principal for The Master Communicator's Writing Services. The Master Communicator's Writing Services provides business communication services to small businesses, non-profits and authors. I am also the mastermind behind the annual Authors Networking Summit (2010–2013), America's Favorite Author Competition and Houston's Favorite Author Competition. I have helped hundreds of authors get their message to the masses through workshops, webinars, my radio show and coaching. I am currently also a senior publishing consultant for the award-winning Ellechor Publishing House.

Known as The Master Communicator, I am proficient in communicating in all forms of media: radio, newspapers, magazines and spoken word. From 2010-2012, I worked as an editor for a major minority communications and marketing company in the fourth largest city in the U.S. (Houston). I hosted the Blog Talk Radio Program, "The Literary Showcase," from 2010 to 2013. I have moved to the HOA platform and host The Literary Fellowship on the third Saturday of each month at 10:00 am. My love for "authorpreneurs" inspires me to take great leaps in finding and creating tools that work for the modern 21st-century author. When asked what love has to do with anything, my response is always, "everything."

Websites: www.mcwritingservices.com,
www.sharoncjenkins.com

Shari Joyce
Divine Consultant and Founder & Chief Spiritual Officer

I believe: Personal development precedes business development and that serving my customers, giving time and profits to my community, growing people and helping them realize their full potential leads to success. Mindfulness, sustainability and corporate social responsibility are all connected to corporate America's bottom line. People, planet and profit!

As a resource for my clients, I am a focused leader who enjoys mentoring over managing. I share 20+ years of skill sets with clients including: Business Development, Community Service, Conflict Resolution, Relationship Sales, Project Management/Coordination, Recycling & Repurposing and Personal Coaching. Today I have a boutique consulting business, Divine Consultant, where I support the growth of companies through cost effective and efficient sales and marketing innovations. I also offer "The New MidLife" coaching to private individuals so what we have called "middle age" may be viewed as a magical turning point while one phase of life transitions into another.

My vision is to be a leading authority on face-to-face selling principles, concepts and techniques while recognizing the Divine in all. My ideas, information and tools create a foundation to support growth while individuals become more effective. By doing so, they offer greater value, enjoy higher incomes and improve their quality of life and the quality of life of those around them.

When I am not working hard, I spend quality time with my family. I enjoy walking in the outdoors. As a previous race walker, I have completed both the Mayors Midnight Sun Marathon in Alaska and the Disney World Marathon in Florida while raising money for the Leukemia & Lymphoma Society.

My education includes a Bachelor of Arts in Spiritual Studies from Emerson Theological Institute in, Oakhurst. CA; Practitioner, Religious Science Church; and Certificates in Mediation: Mediation and Restitution Services (MARS), The San Diego City Attorney Dispute Resolution Office and The Victim Offender Reconciliation Program (VORP).

Website: www.divineconsultant.com

Sandy Kamel
Advocare® Independent Distributor

A Dallas native, I am an independent distributor with Advocare. After years of fighting fatigue, I found new vitality in Advocare's top-selling product, Spark. When I discovered the financial opportunities involved with Advocare, I jumped at the chance to merge my passion for helping others with world-class Advocare products and embracing new entrepreneurial possibilities. Since 1993, AdvoCare has been a world-class nutrition company specializing in health and wellness, weight management, energy and sports performance. Our products are formulated by an elite Scientific and Medical Advisory Board with over 200 years' combined experience in pharmacology, toxicology, nutrition, sports performance and pediatrics. We have a multitude of product endorsers that include professional athletes, champion amateur athletes and acclaimed entertainers. What really makes Advocare stand out, however, is the values upon which it was founded, beginning with placing faith, family and friends above all else. As the foundation of a great life and company, integrity remains at the center of Advocare's leadership. I am proud to be a part of this company, and I am blessed to have the opportunity to collaborate with such like-minded leaders as Shelley.

Websites: www.kameladvocare.com, www.Advo.Life

Rachel Parker
Strategic Communications Consultant

I am in the communications field from a more strategic standpoint. We help clients be very strategic about how they are using their blogs and their e-newsletters and make sure that they all work together to establish relationships with clients and prospects.

Website: www.resonancecontent.com

Carra Riley
Realtor

I am a fun-loving digital player, REALTOR since 1979 and best-selling author who continues to be a life-long learner. I help people "connect the dots" in the Cosmic Cow Pie of life as a consultant for small business and real estate, along with providing custom workshops and seminars.

My real estate experience includes top-producing agent with Moore & Company (350 agents) in Denver, Colorado; broker/owner at Metro Brokers Riley and Company in Westminster, Colorado; Maui Tropical Connections ltd. in Maui, Hawaii and Colorado Real Estate Connections ltd. in Westminster, Colorado. My husband, Tom, and I were group owners at Prestige Real Estate Group in Boulder, Colorado.

I spent 12 years in Arizona, living in Williams - known as the "Gateway to the Grand Canyon" - and selling with creative real estate companies. I currently have my Colorado Brokers license with Realty One Group Premier.

I am a former GRI Instructor for the Colorado Association of Realtors and have CRS, GRI and CRB designations. I got my education at Colorado State University with a degree in Merchandising, which I received in 1974.

I use humor and "real life" experience to engage audiences with both direct selling and Brokerage lessons. My teaching style in the classroom encourages participation, which I believe is an essential component for attendees to be able to absorb the valuable information and take their performance to the next level.

I started my social media journey in 2009 and can be found all over cyberspace on Facebook, Google+, Pinterest, Instagram, Tumblr, Twitter and YouTube.

Google+: https://plus.google.com/+CarraRiley/about

Shelley Roth
President, Springboard Ventures Inc.
Social Media Consultant, Speaker, Trainer, Author

I am a serial entrepreneur and social media trainer, speaker, consultant and author helping individuals, organizations and teams improve marketing effectiveness and sales results via social media. I have a B.S. in Education and hold M.Eds. in Educational Psychology and Educational Administration.

My third book, *Givie to Grow: 9 Principles for Conscious Business, Social Media and Life*, shares top social media strategies used to help thousands of businesses accelerate. These principles are the basis of the newest workshops and speaking topics I am delivering. Applying these practices, I have helped and watched countless businesses increase engagement, grow relationships and accelerate growth using social media. The latest social media workshops and speaking topics based on this book are:

- "Give to Grow" - Level The Playing Field Using Social Media
- From Scarcity to Abundance - Learn to Attract Growth for Your Business
- Reinventing Company Assets - People Over Profits

My books are available on Amazon via www.amazon.com/author/shelleyroth.

I love dogs, cats, people, nature and wildlife.

Visit my social media portal for a calendar of events and social media properties, including Facebook, LinkedIn, YouTube and more: www.shelleyroth.com.

Ronda Suder
Filmmaker, Writer, Actress, Entrepreneur

I am a filmmaker, writer, actress and entrepreneur with a Masters in Human Resources and Industrial Relations. I inspire and empower people through relatable stories reflecting the human condition.

Website: www.rondasuder.com

Pam Terry
Speaker Coach

I am a speaker coach who helps people become confident speakers. I help them with overcoming whatever it is they have to do to be the speaker they want to be. I help them become in demand and position themselves as an expert. Public speaking is one of those opportunities where you have a chance to inspire and motivate others. You are not trying to sell anything: You are trying to alter people's life in some way - make them better.

Website: www.pamterry.com

Deb Tummins
President, Deb Tummins Coaching, LLC

I formed Deb Tummins Coaching, LLC in 2013 as an executive and business coaching practice. The focus of my company is engaging with successful executives and business owners who seek continuous growth in effectiveness and fulfillment.

Prior to starting my own business, I served in various leadership and executive management positions in the high tech industry for over 20 years, working for AT&T, IBM, BMC Software, Traq Wireless and CA Technologies. I have been consistently recognized for my track record as a successful field sales leader and executive, highly capable of driving revenue and business growth through enabling highly effective organizations. I have built and led teams with revenue targets of up to $1.8 billion, up to 1,500 employees and over 7,000 customers.

Through my career, I have developed a wealth of knowledge and experience in leadership recruitment and development, organizational change management, sales organization design and go-to market strategy, compensation planning and client satisfaction. I have served as a key executive in many corporate strategy and planning initiatives involving restructuring, consolidation, P&L planning, and talent assessment and development.

Throughout my career, my passion has been that of recruiting and developing highly effective leadership teams. I especially enjoy working with women who seek to maximize their effectiveness in their careers.

I am a certified Birkman Methodology Consultant, Social and Emotional Intelligence Consultant from ISEI and High Performance Coach from Brendon Burchard's High Performance Coaching Program. I received an MBA from Penn State University and an M.S. Ed. and B.S. Ed. from The University of Memphis.

I am a board member and chair of Vecino Health Centers, a non-profit organization focused on providing quality medical treatment to individuals in underserved communities in Houston. I am also a member of several organizations that promote public spaces: Memorial Park Conservancy, Hermann Park Conservancy and Buffalo Bayou Partnership. I am an avid sports fan of both collegiate and professional teams. I personally enjoy golf, yoga, working out, hiking, travel, photography and entertaining family and friends.

Website: www.debtummins.com

J-Coby Wayne
Agent of Evolution

I am an agent of evolution. As an agent of evolution, it's one of my greatest honors and privileges to realize the opportunity to co-found and steward a number of different world collaboratives as part of my purpose and contribution to helping make the world a better place. These world collaboratives help humanity, our planet and all lives thrive and evolve together through the world of energy by bringing three major world ideas to life: 1) there is a world collaborative guiding evolution 2) everything is energy, evolving together through energy 3) collaboratives built on the expanded and shared reality of the world of energy help the world progress together. World of energy collaboratives like this that I have helped build include: service communities, special online events such as the quarterly Weeks of World Cooperation and opportunities to collaborate with and help support people and projects that are doing good.

As a world traveler and lifelong avid student of culture, civilization and international relations, I always sensed there was more to life than meets the eye and that we are one human family sharing one planet and cosmos that transcends national borders. My early childhood experience seeing the movie, "Star Wars", reinforced the universal human and energy realities and truths I always sensed and set me on a path aspiring to be a real-life Jedi Knight dedicated to living a noble and adventurous life in service of world progress and goodwill for all.

While I have several advanced degrees from Ivy League schools (which I appreciate very deeply) and had a lot of high-profile professional experience and "success" in the high-tech world early on in my post-student life, it's a lifelong identity as a world citizen and a youthful spirit that continually seeks out and recognizes the inherent magic and elegant underlying structure of life and the natural world that I value most as the most significant influences in shaping the appreciations, contributions and collaborations I've been lucky to experience, receive and share in life. I live Amelia Earhardt's quote, *"Adventure is worthwhile in itself"*.

Website: jcobywayne.com

GRATEFUL ACKNOWLEDGEMENTS

I want to acknowledge again the team that made this book happen. First, my awesome editor, J-Coby Wayne and her partner, Kain Sanderson. Without their guidance and confidence in me, this book would not have happened. Next, Heather Swick, who helped with creating some of the exercises, interviewed many of the companies in the book and transcribed the 9 Hangouts we did on Google+. What a great contribution! And, of course, all of the panelists who gave of their time and knowledge and spirit and the people who joined in the live Hangouts. And, finally, Buddy, the Corgi dog and my VP of Morale; without his faithful nature, this book would never have arrived!

www.ingramcontent.com/pod-product-compliance
Lightning Source LLC
Chambersburg PA
CBHW061157240326
R18026500001B/R180265PG41519CBX00026B/45
9780983870449